the complete guide to roots style guitar

by Rick Rossano

Includes Descriptive Audio and Play-Along Tracks in New Orleans, Jump Blues, Rhumba, Country and Funky Blues Styles

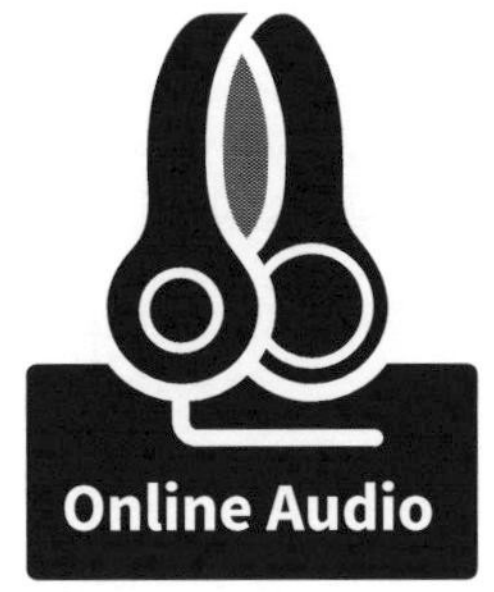

www.melbay.com/31094MEB

Cover image of the T186MX Classic Thinline Electric Guitar is courtesy of Eastman Music Company.

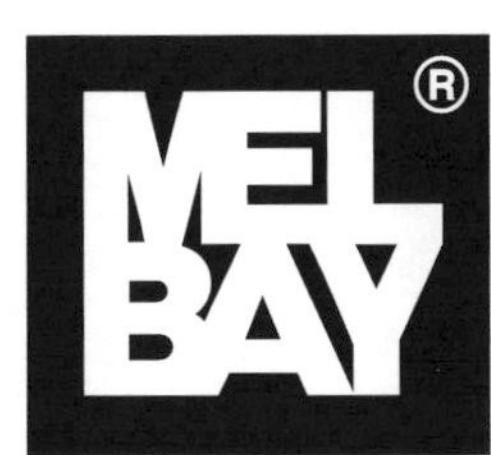

WWW.MELBAY.COM

Foreword

Thank you for purchasing *The Complete Guide to Roots Guitar.* This book contains an easy-to-follow outline for developing both rhythm guitar and soloing vocabularies based on the elements of different roots guitar styles.

We will examine these elements as they relate to rhythm guitar playing and soloing in general, and then look at tips on directly applying them to blues and blues sub-genres: jump blues, New Orleans and Latin/rhumba blues, as well as rockabilly, surf, and country styles.

Contents

CHAPTER 1: FUNDAMENTALS

YOUR SOUND – Amp, Guitar and Effects Settings

AMPS

Most roots guitar styles could be covered with different kinds of amps but traditionally, tube amps have been the model of choice for most guitarists. They have a warm, natural sound that lends itself perfectly to roots guitar styles. There are, however, a ton of modeling or hybrid (preamp tube sections with transistor power amp sections) amps that do a pretty great job of modeling tube amp circuitry and sound. Amp designers have gotten close to having realistic tube "sag" in some modeling amps features.

I'm a tube guy personally for playing live, though I will use amp models for home recording because of convenience. For gigs and at home playing, I use a *Fender* Black Panel Deluxe Reverb. The reverb settings I use vary depending on the acoustics of the room. If it's carpeted or dead, I'll set it around 4 or 5. If it's a "live" room with lots of hard surfaces, I'll back it down to 2 or 3, or maybe play with no reverb. Generally speaking, I don't crank the reverb unless I'm playing surf music.

GUITARS

My guitar settings also vary with the mood; remember that the front (neck) pickup will have a smoother/fatter tone. Conversely, the back/bridge pickup has a sharper, more biting tone. Guitars with a middle pickup have a more midrange sound; those with a three-way toggle switch for two pickups can mix front and back proportionately using the individual pickup's volume knob.

I highly recommend getting acclimated enough with your pickup switch and volume and tone knobs that you can change back and forth freely and on the fly as the vibe of the song or your solo might dictate. With a little practice it will become second nature. If you're blessed enough to have different brands of guitars, one challenge is that a *Gibson* or *Epiphone* will have controls in different locations than *Fender* models do, so it pays to get a feel for where the controls are so that you don't have to stop and stare at your ax in the heat of the battle.

EFFECTS

An enormous range of effects is available on the market today. There are overdrives, distortions and fuzzes which push or drive your signal making it break up and grind; there are modulation-types of effects – tremolo, vibrato, phase, flange, chorus - which create volume, pitch and tone variances; there are also echo, delay and reverb effects which affect the spatial or ambient quality of your guitar's signal.

Moving forward to individual sub-genres of roots guitar styles, I'll make some recommendations of effects traditionally applied to best compliment and augment each style.

TECHNIQUE – Listening and Dynamics, Left and Right-Hand Techinques

LISTENING AND DYNAMICS

There's a reason I mention this first – what makes a musician a GREAT musician is sensitivity to the musical environment they are in and playing not only what is appropriate at any given time, but also at an appropriate volume and with consideration of what others are playing. We want to serve the song.

Whether playing rhythm or soloing, be aware of an element in music referred to as "dynamics". **Dynamics** are the variations (both increases and reductions) in volume, energy levels and musical ideas. Dynamics are applied by individual musicians and are also a band strategy. It's a process of creating musical tension or excitement leading to a resolution or release of that tension. We're telling a musical story through the manipulation of these dynamics. Think of them as applications of "tension and release".

Let's say I start a solo with a simple idea or phrase of 4 or 5 notes. I might begin in a lower register of the scale, maybe at a slightly lower volume. Perhaps I'll repeat the figure every two bars— or apply rests and lay out every two bars. The concept is to gradually increase the intensity of ideas and volume concurrently until, hopefully, a logical conclusion is reached. Don't forget to be conservative with your ideas so that they can last over two or maybe three choruses, or however long your solo section might be. Save the best stuff for last and try to make a tidy exit. Creating a great solo takes practice and is a "big picture" concept.

LEFT-HAND TECHNIQUES

There are lots of left-hand techniques to master that will make your playing a lot more expressive; for example: vibrato, bending, slurring, and hammer-ons and pull-offs.

Vibrato is a pitch variation of the note being held, achieved through a rhythmic pivoting of the left wrist or sometimes left-hand fingers. Let's try an experiment: Hold your left hand straight out with your palm facing down. Now turn your hand so that it is perpendicular to the ground with your thumb facing upward. Do that back and forth slowly, then faster so that you are doing it rapidly, kind of like when you make a "So-So" gesture. That is basically the wrist technique involved in left hand vibrato. Your thumb on the back of the neck and your other left-hand fingers act as ballast around the finger (typically your index) that is applying the vibrato. There are lots of different types of vibratos: B. B. King used a rapid, hummingbird-type vibrato, whereas Albert King used a wide, slower vibrato to give his licks that trademark wobbly sound. Experiment with both extremes and everything in between.

Bending adds a vocal, crying quality to your licks. It's the process of holding a note with the left hand and as it is picked, pushing it up to a higher target note, usually a half step (one fret) or a whole step (two frets) higher. Place two or three fingers of the left hand on the string you are bending to get sufficient "torque" to push the note up to the target pitch. A great exercise to hone your intonation when practicing bending is to play the fretted "target note" first, then bend up to it, then release and compare it to the target note to see if the two are the same. It takes some practice but soon enough your left hand will develop some muscle memory and feel the amount of pressure needed, along with your ear helping to guide it to the target. Typically, most bending happens on the E, B & G strings, though any string can be bent.

Notice how the journey from the initial picked note to the target note creates a period of tension followed by the resolution or release when returning to the picked note. There's that phenomenon of "tension and release" mentioned earlier. It's achieved through bending, through volume dynamics, and through strategic placement of altered chords followed by harmonic resolution. Mastering this technique will make an explosive change in the way you affect your listeners, and if that listener is only you, you will still be blown away by these applications of sonic subterfuge. Really good stuff, **with more to come!**

A **slide** is the cousin of a bend – the technique of sliding up or down to a target note can be very effective. You pick the first note, then drag it to the target note without letting it die out. A slide could be a half step (one fret) or a whole step (two frets) or even more. Triplets can be created by playing a note and sliding it up and back down, only picking it once at the beginning of the triplet phrase. There are lots of cool ways to apply this technique.

HAMMER-ONS AND PULL-OFFS

These two techniques are mirror images of each other. The **hammer-on** is played by picking the first note of a lick (typically held with the index finger of the left hand) and hammering on a second higher note on the same string (usually done with the middle or ring finger of the left hand, depending on the interval of the hammered note). The second note is NOT picked. A great example is the hammering-on of a major third after playing a minor third inside a minor pentatonic scale– another example of the tension and release theory. Using a minor pentatonic scale in the key of A at the fifth fret, we would pick a C note on the fifth fret of the G string, followed by a hammer-on at the 6th fret of the G string, going from a temporary minor third and resolving to the major third. That's another nice "tension and release" move.

Listen to audio track 1 to hear a minor 3rd to major 3rd hammer-on played to a I-IV-V 12-bar track.

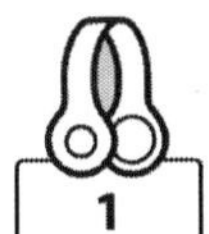

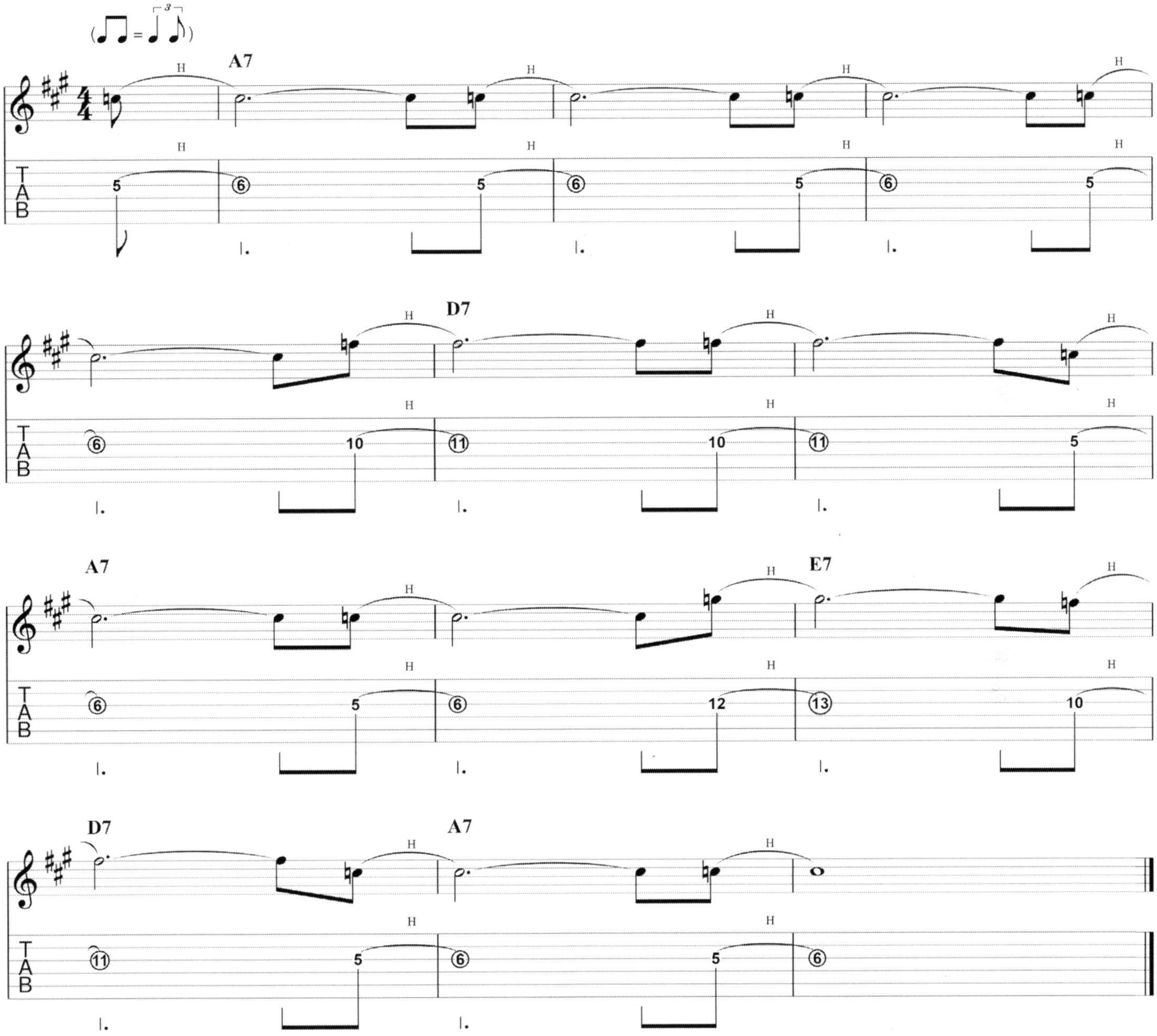

The **pull-off** is basically the same move as a hammer-on, in reverse. Staying in the same A minor pentatonic box, we might pick the 8th fret of the B string (a flatted 7th or G note) holding it with our ring finger, then holding an E note at the fifth fret of the same B string with our index finger, pull the note off with a snapping motion to resolve the pull-off at the fifth fret. Like the hammer-on, the first note is picked, but the second note is not. A great exercise to master the pull-off is to go through the pentatonic scale (two notes per string) one string at a time, picking the top note of each given string then pulling off to the lower note of that string. You'll build some callouses getting this one together.

Listen to audio track 2 to hear the pull-off technique applied to the minor pentatonic scale in A, starting on the C note at the 8th fret on the high-E string and ending on the A note at the 5th of the low-E string.

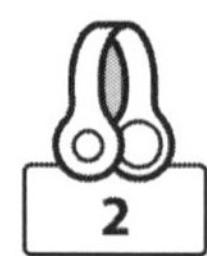

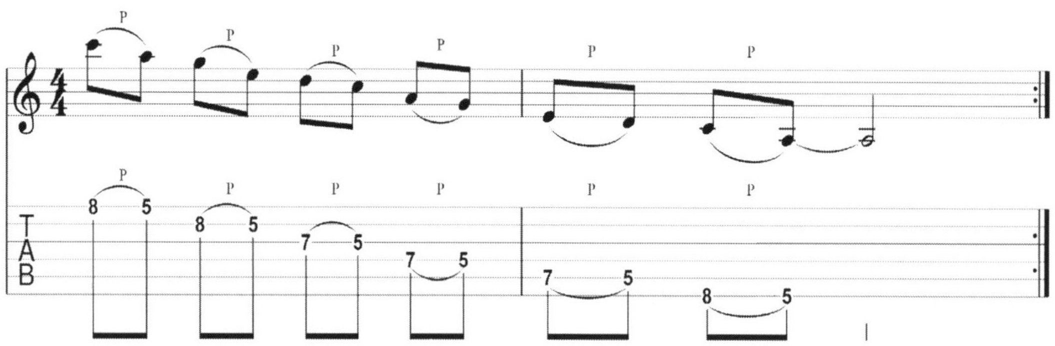

RIGHT HAND

There are tons of right-hand techniques to explore: strumming, picking, muting, raking, fingerpicking, and so on.

Strumming – Try to develop the habit of using an even stroke when practicing your strumming. It might sound obvious but making sure that your down-stroke (typically played on the downbeat) and upstroke (played on the upbeat) are **even** in terms of rhythm and volume— is not as easy as it sounds. Using a metronome or drum loop (tons of free ones on YouTube) is a great regulator for getting your rhythm chops together. The same goes for practicing scales and single-note lines, though some notes get emphasized more than others when soloing. As far as woodshedding for consistency and evenness, a beat-keeper is essential for effective practice.

Muting is a technique achieved by lightly resting the base or heel of your right palm across the strings immediately in front of the bridge. This is a great way to control volume, tone and dynamics without having to stop and reach for the volume or tone knob. Practice placing your right hand on or right in front of the bridge; there's literally about a half- inch shift that will greatly affect the tonal quality and loudness of your sound. It's a killer right-hand technique for varying dynamics.

Raking is a technique that combines muting with a downward or upward pick-stroke across adjacent strings that precedes the target note with a percussive, scraping sound. It's widely used in blues, rock and most roots styles. It will give your phrases and licks a unique, expressive quality.

Phrasing is the timing and shaping of notes and rests of different duration. Your choice of notes, the sequence in which you play them, the dynamics and emphasis given to each note – are all elements of phrasing. Think of the way you tell a joke; the use of time, space, tension, and the way a punchline is delivered. Phrasing can take its time, or be frenzied, be smooth and even, or played ahead or behind the beat. Hopefully all of the facets of phrasing are applied when you create an interesting, dynamic solo.

When we begin to combine all of the above-mentioned techniques – vibrato, bending, slurring, using muting, raking and dynamics in your phrasing – you'll really start to hear your instrument "speak" as opposed to sounding like you are just walking up and down scales and exercises. These are the tools you'll collect and apply to bring your ideas and personality to life on your guitar.

Application of Sound and Techniques for Roots Guitar Styles

Now that we've reviewed some of the basic elements of guitar sounds and techniques, let's dial them in as they apply to the different sub-genres of roots guitar styles. I'll make some suggestions for you to try out and hopefully, you'll find some ideas in here that will help you to hone your skills and give you a new perspective or two. Let's go!

BLUES

"Blues came from the South", to quote the great Al Anderson, and Texas, and Chicago, Detroit, and New York and Louisiana. The blues is really the source of all roots music. The template – meaning the 12-bar set of chord changes typically used in the form – is the same. Really, only feel and groove are the main differences between the various roots styles, whether we're talking blues and rockabilly, surf, or country.

YOUR SOUND – Your blues-approved sound should have a bit of "hair" on it. By the book, it's called overdrive or distortion, but we're definitely not talking about heavy metal grind here. Just a nice tube-like breakup when you lean into things to add a little edge to your solos. As far as effects go, try not to fall victim to overkill. Muddy would be flipping in his grave if he heard a helicopter-flanger or a psychedelic Echoplex freakout on your solo.

There's a famous Howlin' Wolf quote related by the late session guitarist Pete Cosey: At an ill-advised psychedelic album session with *Chess* records attempting to cash-in on the acid rock craze at the time, Wolf asked Pete, "Why don't you take that (expletive) wow-wow pedal and throw it into the lake on your way to get a haircut?"

TECHNIQUE – Keep in mind that some of the techniques we talked about— namely, bending and vibrato—are two biggies when it comes to blues guitar technique; in the right hand, muting and raking are in that same category. Hit it and MEAN it.

INFLUENCES TO CHECK OUT: B. B. King, Albert King, Freddie King, Albert Collins, Otis Rush, Lightnin' Hopkins, John Lee Hooker, Muddy, Jimmy Reed, T-Bone Walker, Lazy Lester and early Johnny "Guitar" Watson.

ROCKABILLY

came blasting out of sheds and garages in the early 50s with equal parts of hopped-up hillbilly twang and Delta Blues stomp. It was a welcome response to the limp state of popular music of the time. Rockabilly continues to this day to be a vital and hard rockin' musical form.

YOUR SOUND – I prefer to run my amp pretty clean for rockabilly. I'll usually dial in a mid-to-trebly tone on my guitar and use right-hand muting to control tone on the fly. The reason I use a sound with more treble is that once you dial-in the prerequisite slap-back delay, a rhythm or neck pickup will tend to muddy-up. You can hear slap-back delay/echo on recordings all the way back to Scotty Moore on the essential early Elvis sides – ground zero for rockabilly guitar – up through contemporary players like Brian Setzer and Jim Heath (The Reverend Horton Heat). Both Brian and Jim are tape-echo purists. The old Echoplex units have a preamp stage in their circuitry that adds a nice little sting to the guitar signal. If you can get one, they sound killer but there is a matter of maintenance – cleaning the tape heads and having some backup tape cartridges. The current batch of delays out there include analog builds that actually have variable wobble, and high-end roll-off to emulate the cranky old tape units. A digital pedal, however, will get you 99% of the way there. As too many repeats end up sounding soupy, setting up a single repeat on the pedal at anywhere from 80 to 120 milliseconds should do the job.

TECHNIQUE – Double stops are a left-hand technique that goes with rockabilly like peanut butter goes with bananas, at least according to Elvis. The minor pentatonic scales rule here, and double stops fit this scale like a glove. If you look at the typical minor pentatonic and blues "boxes" or diagrams later in this book, you'll note that the identical pattern on the E, B & G strings lends itself perfectly for spinning out double-stop Chuck Berry-style licks. Higher strings sound cleaner for double stops, but they get muddy on the lower strings. If there is a whammy bar/ tremolo/"talent lever" on your guitar, a sprinkling of nervous whammy wiggles will add a nice sheen to your solos! No dive bombs, please.

INFLUENCES TO CHECK OUT: Scotty Moore (Elvis' *Sun Records* singles), Paul Burlison (Rock and Roll Trio), Joe Maphis, Larry Collins (The Collins Kids), Merle Travis, Carl Perkins, and Sonny Curtis (Buddy Holly).

SURF

Surf guitar originated in the late 50s in Southern California, allegedly as an attempt to emulate the crashing sound of waves. It was primarily started by the "Sultan of Surf", Mr. Richard Monsour. (You may know him by the moniker Dick Dale). Surf guitar was built from equal parts of Middle Eastern and Mexican melodies, machine-gun right-hand picking and a dripping spring reverb originally designed by the Hammond organ company, which eventually, fortuitously migrated into Fender guitar amplifiers.

YOUR SOUND – We want to run about a 90-percent clean sound for our surf guitar amp platform. By the way, learning the varied degrees of amp cleanliness/dirtiness will serve you well; getting to know how your amp performs at different settings will help you to make it behave exactly the way you want. Reverb is your friend when it comes to effects that are surf-appropriate. Hardcore surf guitarists insist on the free-standing *Fender* Reverb Unit for the ultimate reverb splash-fest, but most *Fender* amps have a very respectable reverb available. I crank the reverb on my *Deluxe Reverb* to 6 or 7, depending on the room and condition of the tubes.

Another crucial effect for surf guitar is tremolo or vibrato (the effect, not the technique). Tremolo is a volume oscillation that comes in many *Fender* amps, it can be set to be rhythmically in sync with the tempo of the tune you are playing, which is a neat trick. Vibrato (again the effect, not the technique) is a pitch oscillation effect, the rate and depth being adjustable in the same way as tremolo. Both sound epic in conjunction with reverb. Gnarly, dude!

TECHNIQUE – In roots-style guitar approaches, less is more – and especially so in traditional surf. You generally don't hear maximum shredding, notwithstanding Dick Dale. You can safely bet that the good ol' minor pentatonic scale (see pages 48-49) will cover most of the heavy lifting for your soloing needs. The blues scale (a modified minor pentatonic scale) will work nicely too, but don't shoot for a blues vibe or feel. You have to respect the domain. A big part of the appeal of many of the great surf/instro [instrumental] records is the unbridled joy and enthusiasm of the bands—for example, all of the one-hit-wonder (but no less important) bands like *The Lively Ones, The Marketts, The Tornadoes, The Surfaris*, and on and on.

Muting is a technique you hear used extensively on surf recordings. Try taking any simple 3 or 4-note riff, jack up the reverb to splooshy levels and apply the muting technique lightly resting the side of your hand on the strings near the bridge. Instant cowabunga!

Another oft-used trick is the **gliss** (short for glissando). A prime example of this technique is the immortal intro to the surf monster "Pipeline" by *The Chantays* from 1963. Do a *YouTube* search for their appearance on the Lawrence Welk show, a mindblower. A gliss is a rhythmic device in which the right hand rapidly picks a string while muting it; in this case the left hand also does the muting, holding but not actually fretting the note. The left hand randomly starts up high on the fretboard, usually on the low E string. Unquestionably, Dick Dale is the king of the gliss. It takes a good amount of practice to do it well but it is worth the effort and should be part of any respectable surf guitarist's bag of tricks.

A third cool surf technique is the application of the **whammy bar.** No dive-bombing here either por favor – we are shooting for a more gentle, Hawaiian-style vibe. Most effective on chords. Tubular!

INFLUENCES TO CHECK OUT: Dick Dale, Nokie Edwards (The Ventures), Link Wray, Duane Eddy, Hank Marvin (The Shadows), Bob Demmon (The Astronauts), Paul Johnson (The Bel-Aires), Jim Fuller (The Surfaris), and Bobby Fuller (Bobby Fuller Four).

COUNTRY

YOUR SOUND – In country music, I shoot for the cleanest amp sound/tones possible. We're still talking about tube-amp sound, so it's still not "clinically" clean. Again, I'll add a bit of **reverb** for ambiance. Another cool trick is to sync a bit of delay to lock-in with the tempo of the tune we're playing. A little **compression**—another stomp box you need— adds a snappy feel that sounds great for country. My personal guitar of choice is the trusty *Telecaster*; a favorite of guys from Luther Perkins and Don Rich and Buck Owens, to Brad Paisley. It has serious twang-ability and is tough to beat tone-wise. Any *Fender* is great, but an overlooked fact is that a lot of country players used *Jazzmasters* back in the day. Nothing wrong with other guitars either. If you're using a humbucker-equipped guitar, you can get a respectable tone by using the middle pickup switch setting and dialing the neck pickup back a bit.

TECHNIQUE – For country soloing both the major pentatonic and the mixolydian scales are great roadmaps (see diagrams to follow). They lend themselves to both half and whole-step bending. I recommend integrating your right-hand fingers with your pick for both rhythm and soloing wherever possible. It's a feel thing. Obviously, you can't flat-pick bluegrass without a flat-pick – but there's something about the sound and feel of your fingers for manipulating licks and partial chords that I just can't get with a pick. Kudos to my pal the great Gary Hooker with Brad Paisley's band for the inspiration and guidance down that path.

There's a neat right-hand picking trick (Yes, it's OK to pick up your pick again!) called a **false harmonic** that generates a kind of overtone. To achieve it, you use only the tiniest amount of pick sticking out between the thumb and first finger of your right hand; the idea is to barely brush the picked string with the flesh of the thumb-tip or fingertip immediately after the pick hits the string. Experiment with the location of your picking position relative to the bridge of the guitar. The distance from the bridge and fretted note, as well as the ration of pick to flesh, affects the results you'll get, so do some experimenting. Danny Gatton and Roy Buchanan were masters of this technique – two astonishing guitarists who used Telecasters, and blurred the lines between blues, country, rockabilly and jazz.

INFLUENCES TO CHECK OUT: Roy Clark, Jerry Reed, Chet Atkins, Don Rich (Buck Owens and The Buckaroos), Luther Perkins (Johnny Cash), Clarence White (The Byrds), James Burton (Ricky Nelson, Elvis), and Danny Gatton.

In the end, there are far more similarities between different roots guitar styles than you might have initially thought. Don't be afraid to collect all the bits of theory, technique and information you can from any style of music and try applying it to others. Any musician who says he or she doesn't steal ideas from everywhere they can is either not trying, not telling the truth, or simply missing out on a TON of free inspiration. It's all good, and we can learn from everywhere – from punk to polkas, from steel guitars to saxophones, and most importantly, from each other. Keep on playing and listening!

CHAPTER 2: RHYTHM GUITAR CONCEPTS

As developing guitarists, we initially gather a handful of standard-issue chords to help us navigate our favorite tunes. They get the job done, but sometimes we want to hear something more interesting or compelling, usually after the shelf life has run out on our old reliable chord shapes. The good news is that we're keeping what we know and building on it via tweaks and adjustments. To get started, let's look at one of my favorite shortcuts: the partial chord.

Partial Chords – 6ths & 7ths, and the Freddie Green Method

Partial chords have several useful advantages; through the elimination of redundant notes within a chord, they take up less sonic real estate. They're more concise harmonically and leave more space too, which is a thoughtful courtesy to extend to the soloist/vocalist or other instrumentalists. Secondly, the reduction of notes makes partial chords physically easier to navigate and manipulate, which amounts to less work (Yay!).

Check out the process of getting rid of non-essential notes within a chord: The bass player is typically playing the root or tonic of most chords, so one example of note reduction is that we can take out the bottom note of our chord. If the root or tonic is repeated in the chord—and loads of chords have at least two root or tonic notes in them, sometimes three— some of those root notes can be eliminated as well.

Here's an example: An open E chord has the root at the bottom in the low open-E string. On the second fret of the D string, there's another E or root note, and in the top open-E string, there's a third E root or tonic note. They are not incorrect; they're just kind of redundant, as the bass player is usually covering those root tones anyway.

Sometimes you might take out the lowest root note but keep another tonic/root in the middle of the chord; sometimes you may keep the root on the bottom but thin out the middle of the chord. Think Freddie Green —more on his wizardry later. We **do** want to keep the **third** of the chord, as it determines the important major or minor quality of the chord, and add some type of color, i.e., a 7th, 6th, 9th, or 6 + 7 (13th) to put some *flavoring* on the chord. The sixths and sevenths etc. give personality and vibe to a chord, so we want to add something interesting to give the chord some harmonic vibrancy and depth.

Remember, whatever notes you eliminate from the left hand through those partial chord/note reductions, need to also be eliminated from your right hand. It's a left-hand/right-hand coordinated effort. Go team! Identify and feel out the selected left-hand partial chord notes with the fingers of your right hand to match the new partial chord, then after you have refocused the scope of remaining strings and notes, bring in the pick with your right hand or use right-hand fingers in a claw style. It's fine to use a pick to strum partial chords; you will gradually get used to muting the unnecessary strings with your left-hand fingers. It depends on the feel and tempo of a given tune as to which right-hand technique (pick vs. fingers) you might decide to use.

By modifying a few of the standard chord forms you already use, you can end up with some ultra-portable, killer sounds to apply to different styles of roots guitar. Here are a few examples on the following pages.

Partial 6th and 7th Chords

This example uses something that fits like a glove in all blues styles – partial 6th and 7th chord shapes. For the I chord you could envision it as either the top four strings of an E-shape barré chord re-fingered with an added 6th, or even simpler, as an F chord shape – with an additional added 6th on the B string. The IV and V chords are formed by reducing an A7 barré form to the top four strings only. Everything in the I, IV and V chords here all happens on the top four strings.

Listen to audio track 3 to hear the partial 6th and 7th chords played over a 12-bar blues track.

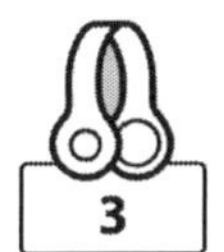

A6 I Chord

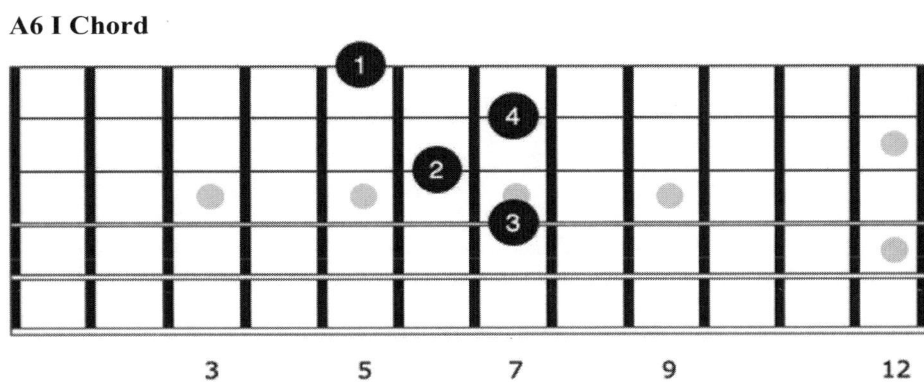

D7 IV Chord

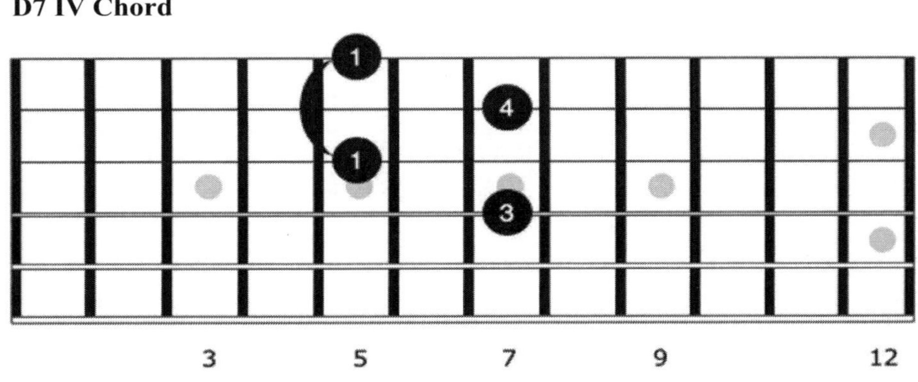

E7 V Chord

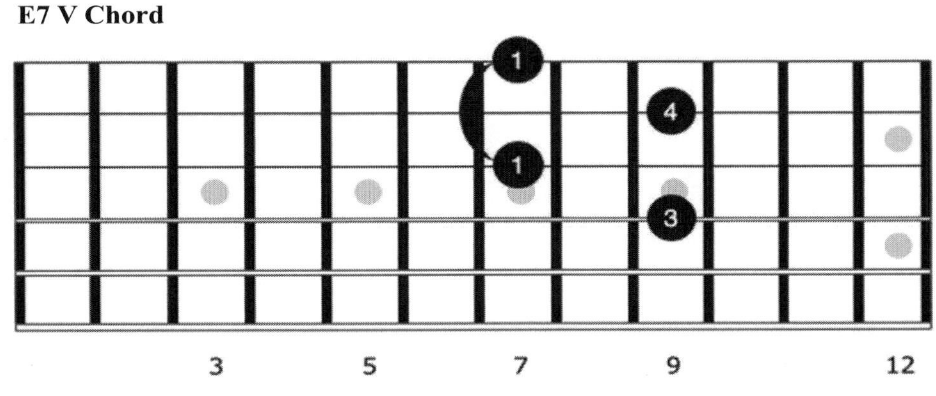

Partial 6th and 7th Chords: Higher Inversions

These next 3-note chords are super portable and extra swank; they bring the flavor of a horn section into your arrangements. They're also voiced higher than the first 6th and 7th chord voicings example, which gives you a brighter sounding option.

For this I or tonic chord, we're using a different inversion of an A6 chord at frets 9, 10 and 11. (See diagram.) Then, by lowering the C-sharp on the 9th fret of the E-string down a half step to the C-natural at the 8th fret, we've created a partial D7 chord (which is the IV of A). To make the V-chord change, you just slide the whole thing up two frets and you've got a E7 (the V of A). I use these little guys a lot.

Listen to audio track 4 to hear partial 6th and 7th chords played over a 12-bar blues track.

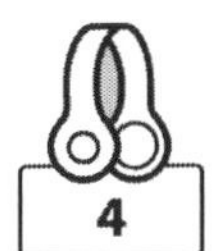

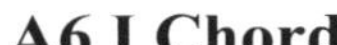

A6 I Chord

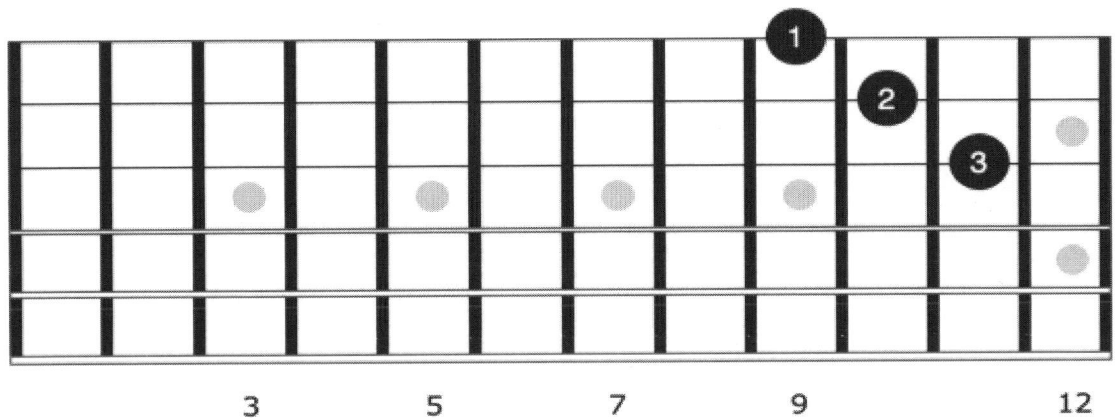

D7 IV Chord

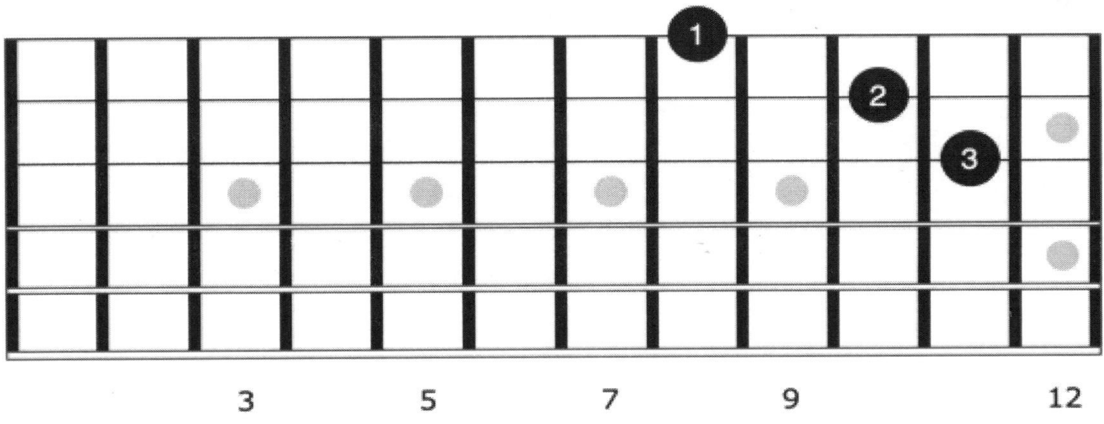

E7 V Chord

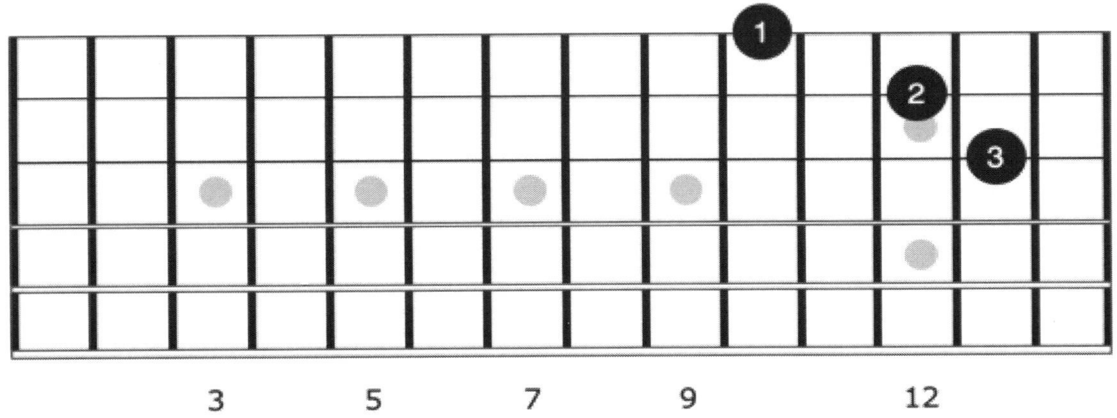

The Freddie Green Partial Chord Method

Our next examples present a quick look at the Freddie Green (1911 – 1987) system. Given his history with The Count Basie Orchestra, Freddie was one of the all-time rhythm guitar monsters in the blues & swing guitar idiom.

Freddie's method places the root on the bottom of the I (A) chord, skips the A string entirely, and places the 7th of the chord on the D string and the third of the chord on the G string **(see diagram).** Then, to move to the IV chord, he keeps the same bass note (A on the 5th fret of the low E string) under the IV chord as a bass note substitute for an inverted V chord. He used this inversion a LOT, giving a chord a fat, hipster flavor! What's really cool is that when we build the rest of that IV chord, the middle notes from the I chord —the 7th, which was on the 5th fret of the D string, and the 3rd which was on the 6th fret of the G string—both get lowered a half step and are now respectively the 3rd (4th fret of the D string) and 7th (5th fret of the G string) of the IV (D9) chord.

This sounds a bit complicated, but the diagram makes it easy to understand. Finally, by simply sliding the whole thing up a whole step from the IV chord (D7), you hit the V chord (E7) in the turnaround, also with that inverted V, now up a whole step with a B on the bottom. Remember, all the while—the bass guitar is reenforcing the roots of the chords, among other notes.

Listen to audio track 5 to hear partial Freddie Green-style chords played over a I-IV-V 12-bar blues track.

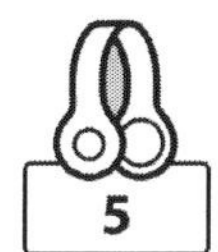

A7 (I Chord)

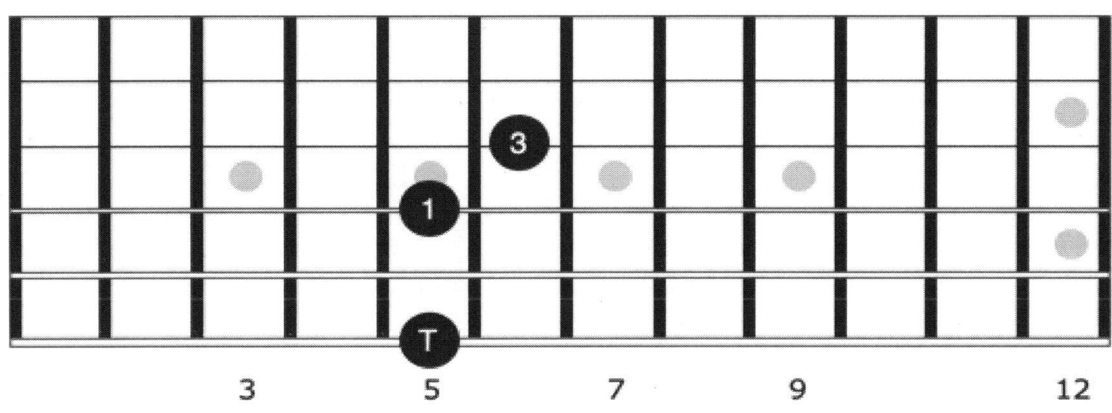

D7/A (IV Chord w/Inverted 5th)

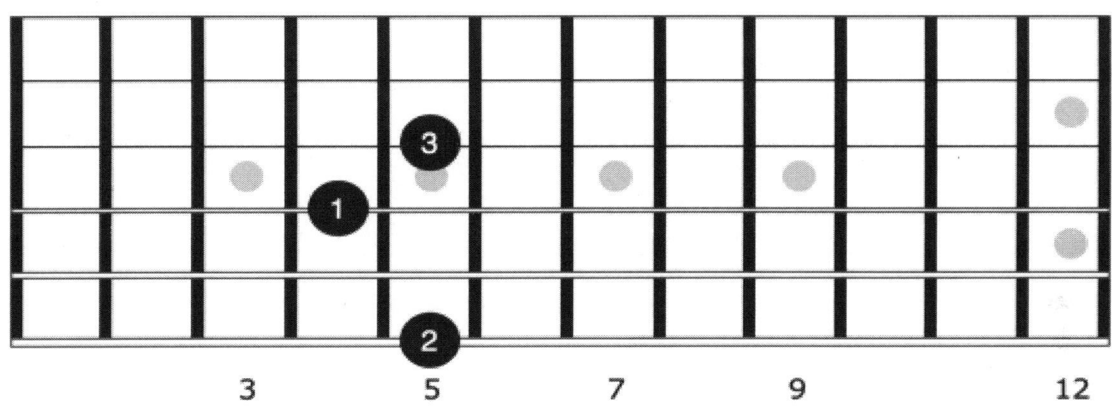

E7/B (V Chord w/Inverted 5th)

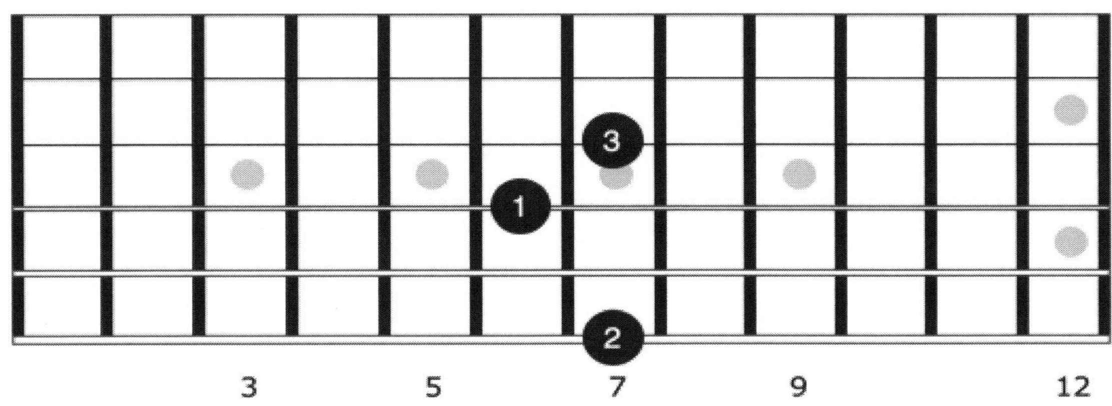

If we were to apply this partial chord system over **an optional ii-V turnaround** in the 9th and 10th bar of a blues form, we'd use a root/7/ flatted-3 chord at the seventh fret (that would be a Bm7) in place of a V chord, and the V chord (inverted V/3/7, that's E9) in place of a IV chord **(see the ii-V diagram).** (More on the ii-V turnaround later.)

Listen to audio track 6 to hear these ii-V chords played over a 12-bar blues track which features a ii-V turnaround.

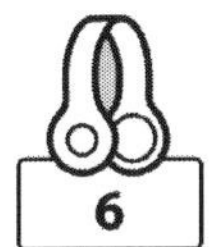

Bm7 (ii Chord)

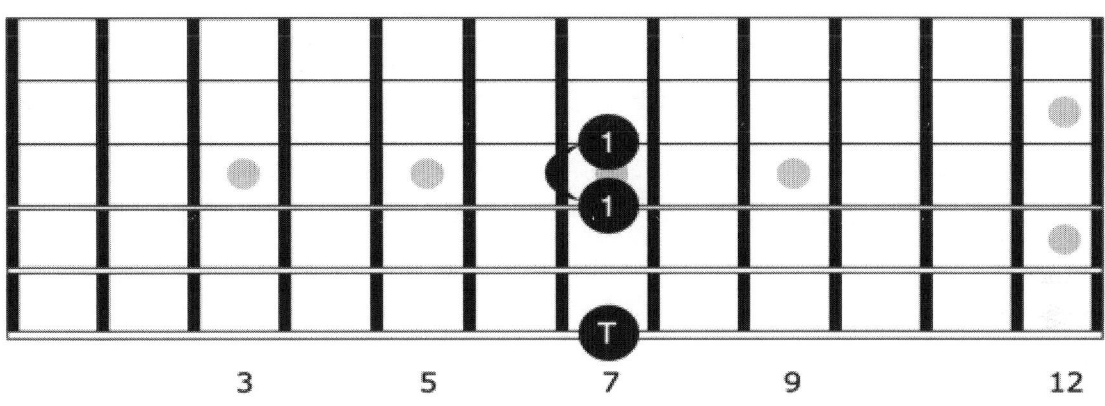

E7/B (V Chord)

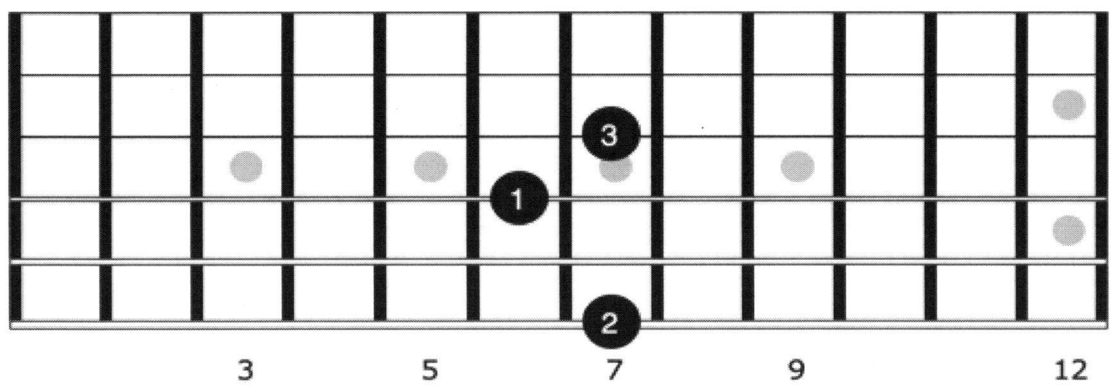

If you're REALLY lazy (like me!), there's a micro version of the Freddie Green system where you can just use the inside 7th & 3rd chord tones for a I-IV-V set of changes by just moving those two notes over a 3-fret span **(see following example).** I call it the "Miracle Mini" chord; it's super useful and an easy grab when you're in a hurry.

Listen to the audio track 7 to hear partial 7th chords played over a I-IV-V 12-bar track.

A7 (I Chord 7th on D string and 3rd on G string)

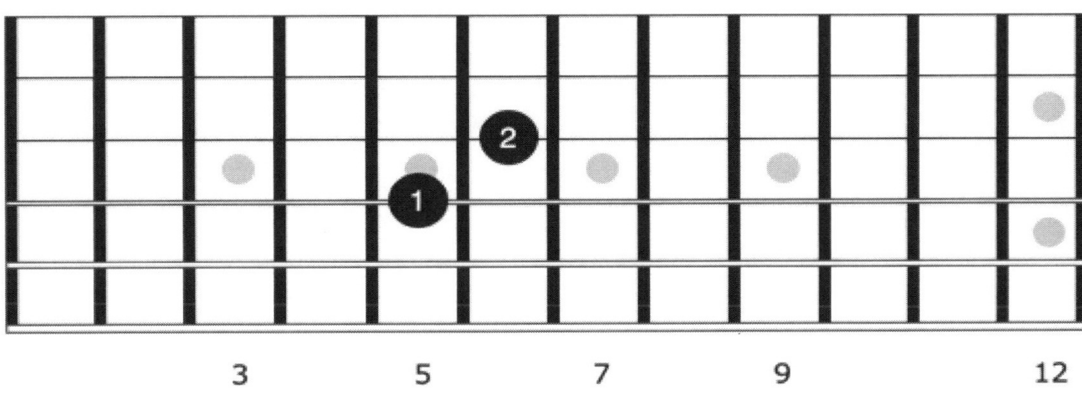

D7 or 9 (IV Chord 3rd on D string 7th on G string)

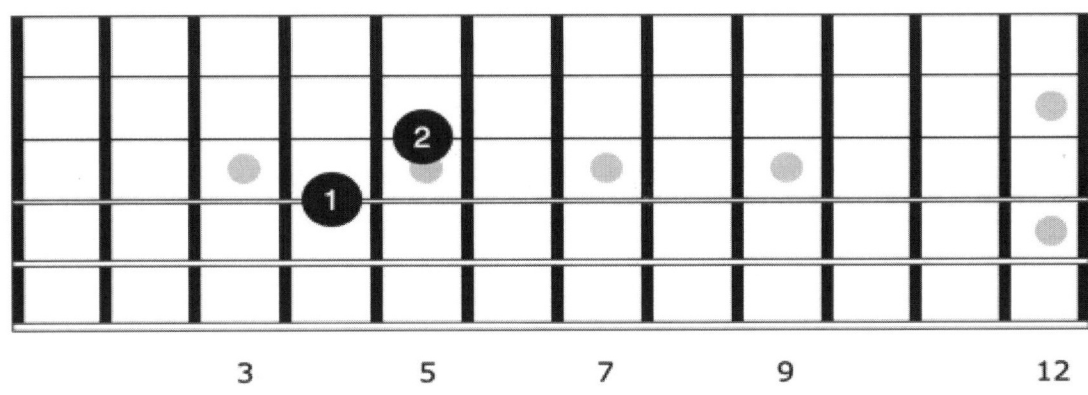

E7 or 9 (V Chord 3rd on D string 7th on G string)

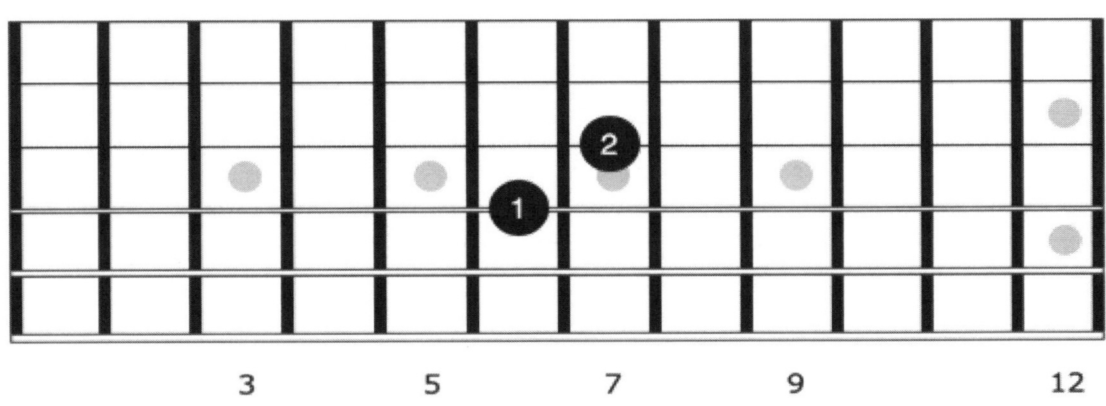

“Grease” Chords, Different Turnarounds and “Funny” (Odd) Chords

The Tension and Release Concept

The practice of creating tension and release or resolution at specific points in a musical structure is a tool that will yield powerful results in your playing. There are small windows of one or two beats as you approach pending chord changes that allow you to temporarily create sonic chaos that transitions into the anticipated chord; this creates a sense of musical relief to the listener, and to the player— if we make the change on time! The transitions inject musical thrills for both our listeners and us as performers. It takes some dedication to master, as the opportunities appear and evaporate pretty quickly – depending on the tempo, they can be challenging to navigate – but the musical payoff is glorious when you get it under your belt!

Half-Step Approaches and Borrowing Beats

A common method for applying this technique is to “borrow” one or two beats from the end of the bar previous to a chord change. So, if we are in the Key of A and are playing a A7 to a D7 change, we would play two beats of A7 then “grease” into the IV chord, by “borrowing” the last two beats of that bar and substituting either a C♯7 or E♭7. Either chord presents a half-step approach to the “target” chord of D7. Both approaches work; either approach will create momentary tension that is released when we land on the upcoming chord change. Try both and apply the one that sounds best to you.

Listen to audio track 8 to hear the half-step approach of “grease” chords played over a 12-bar blues track; the “grease” chord can come from either below or above the intended target chord.

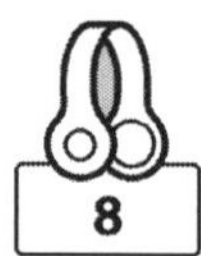

Note that “greasing” an approaching IV chord from ABOVE is technically what’s called a **flat-5 substitution** – you are momentarily superimposing a chord that is an interval of a flatted fifth away from the I (One) chord ON TOP or IN PLACE of the One chord. This substitution is really powerful for creating momentary tension which gets resolved when we land on the approaching IV chord. All the important jazz improvisers —Trane, Miles, Monk, Bird, and Dizzy— used it and contemporary artists still do. The same theory applies to soloing over those momentary windows of tension. Master it, and you will be amazed at how your playing will take a quantum leap in terms of freshness.

“Greasing” or using half-step approaches – from below, or above – will work for **any** chord change to create temporary tension that gets resolved by landing on the approaching target chord. I to IV, IV back to I, I to V, ii to V, V to I… it’s all good! Having said that, it will probably sound fairly demented if we apply it to “Michael Row the Boat Ashore” or “Happy Birthday”, or use it on every single chord change approach, but the “grease” chord technique goes together like peanut butter and jelly in all roots styles.

Half-Step Approach "Grease" Chords

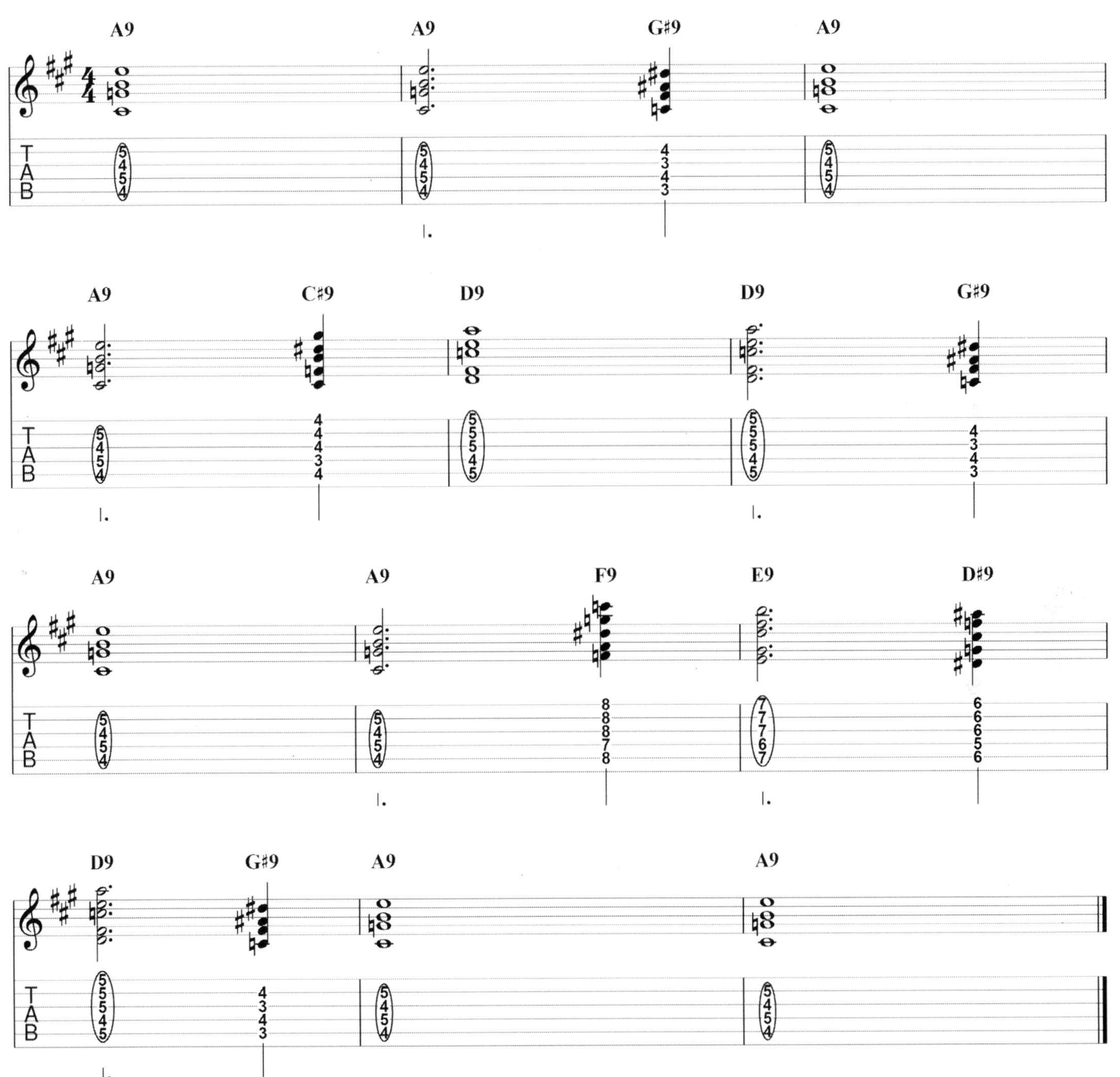

Let's look at some examples in the Nashville Numbering System, first showing a regular I-IV-V 12-bar form with "grease" chord windows:

TWO BASIC 12-BAR FORMS with V-IV-I Turnarounds

Half-Step Approach Using "Grease" Chords

To create tension and release use the last 1 or 2 beats of the previous measure—as shown in **bold**—to approach the next chord change from a half-step below or above:

1) Long I = 4 bars of I

1 1 1 1 / 1 1 1 1 / 1 1 1 1 / 1 1 **1 1**

4 4 4 4 / 4 4 **4 4** / 1 1 1 1 / 1 1 **1 1**

5 5 **5 5** / 4 4 **4 4** / 1 1 **1 1** / 5 5 **5 5**

2) The "Quick IV" = goes quickly to IV in the 2nd bar

1 1 1 1 / 4 4 **4 4** / 1 1 1 1 / 1 1 **1 1**

4 4 4 4 / 4 4 **4 4** / 1 1 1 1 / 1 1 **1 1**

5 5 **5 5** / 4 4 **4 4** / 1 1 **1 1** / 5 5 **5 5**

Different Turnaround Ideas

Let's examine variations of a "ii-V" turnaround. Traditionally, the most basic turnaround in the blues/roots form is a V-IV-I-V. A super basic variation is ending with 2 bars of the I chord in place of that last bar of V. For playing down-in-the-dirt blues, I prefer the primitive sound of a long 1 (one) at the end of a 12-bar form.

A killer turnaround variation is the ii-V turnaround. We substitute a minor ii in place of the normal V in Bar 9 and play a V in place of the IV in the following bar. This sub kills in a jump blues feel and has been widely used in that style for decades. Here's a typical ii-V turnaround substitution:

BASIC 12-BAR FORM with a **Minor ii-V-I** Turnaround

1) Long I = 4 bars of I

1 1 1 1 / 1 1 1 1 / 1 1 1 1 / 1 1 1 1

4 4 4 4 / 4 4 4 4 / 1 1 1 1 / 1 1 1 1

2 2 2 2 / 5 5 5 5 / 1 1 1 1 / 5 5 5 5

2) A "Quick IV" goes quickly to IV in the 2nd bar

1 1 1 1 / 4 4 4 4 / 1 1 1 1 / 1 1 1 1

4 4 4 4 / 4 4 4 4 / 1 1 1 1 / 1 1 1 1

2 2 2 2 / 5 5 5 5 / 1 1 1 1 / 5 5 5 5

The second example shows the same “grease” chord approaches applied to a ii-V turnaround:

TWO BASIC 12-BAR FORMS with Minor ii-V-I Turnarounds Using Half-Step “Grease” Chord Approaches:

To create tension/release, use the last 1 or 2 beats of the bars as shown in bold to approach the next chord change from a half step below or above.

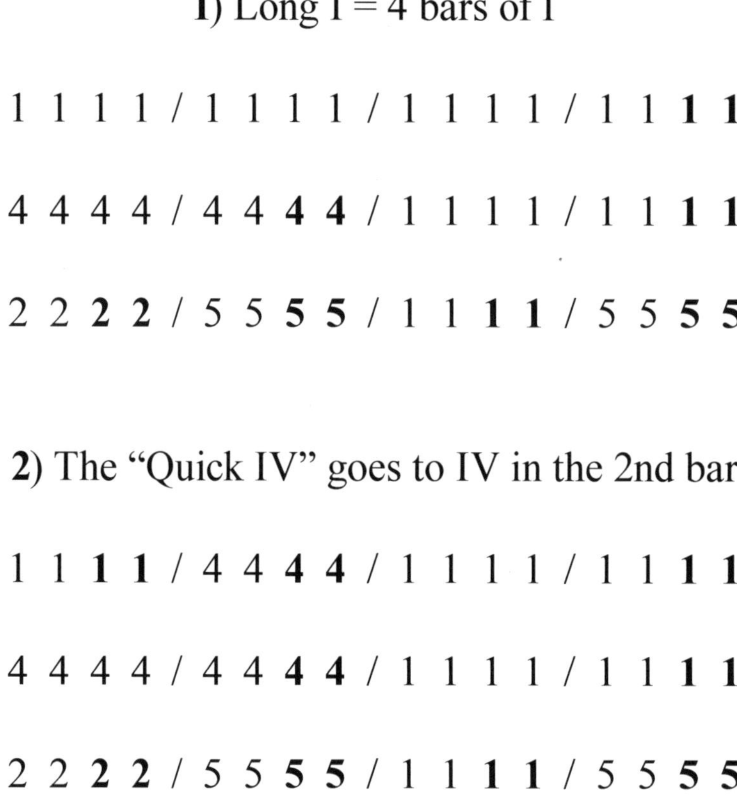

1) Long I = 4 bars of I

1 1 1 1 / 1 1 1 1 / 1 1 1 1 / 1 1 **1 1**

4 4 4 4 / 4 4 **4 4** / 1 1 1 1 / 1 1 **1 1**

2 2 **2 2** / 5 5 **5 5** / 1 1 **1 1** / 5 5 **5 5**

2) The “Quick IV” goes to IV in the 2nd bar

1 1 **1 1** / 4 4 **4 4** / 1 1 1 1 / 1 1 **1 1**

4 4 4 4 / 4 4 **4 4** / 1 1 1 1 / 1 1 **1 1**

2 2 **2 2** / 5 5 **5 5** / 1 1 **1 1** / 5 5 **5 5**

Play along with tracks 41, 42, 44, 45, 47, and 48 for experience with ii-V turnarounds in various keys.

Those “Funny” (Odd) Chords

The use of one or two-beat “windows” for subterfuge (through the application of half-step chord approaches) can be ratcheted up to create even more tension by applying “funny” chords –that is, altered chords that are augmented, diminished or demolished in other nefarious, unusual ways.

A gateway weirdo chord, and one of my favorites is the **diminished chord.** Typically, one spot you might have heard it applied is over the last half of a section of the IV chord. If we are halfway into a 12-bar blues form in A and are playing two bars in a row of the IV chord (in this case, a D7), the second bar or last half of that section of IV could be altered by raising the root of the IV chord a half tone (D to D-sharp) to create a diminished iv chord. **Note that the IV chord MUST contain a flatted-7 for this diminished chord substitution to function correctly.**

Listen to audio track 9 to hear the diminished chord applied over the second bar of the IV chord; typically, the diminished chord is found in bar 6 when played within a 12-bar blues.

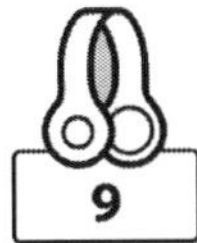

Diminished iv Chord with a Raised Root

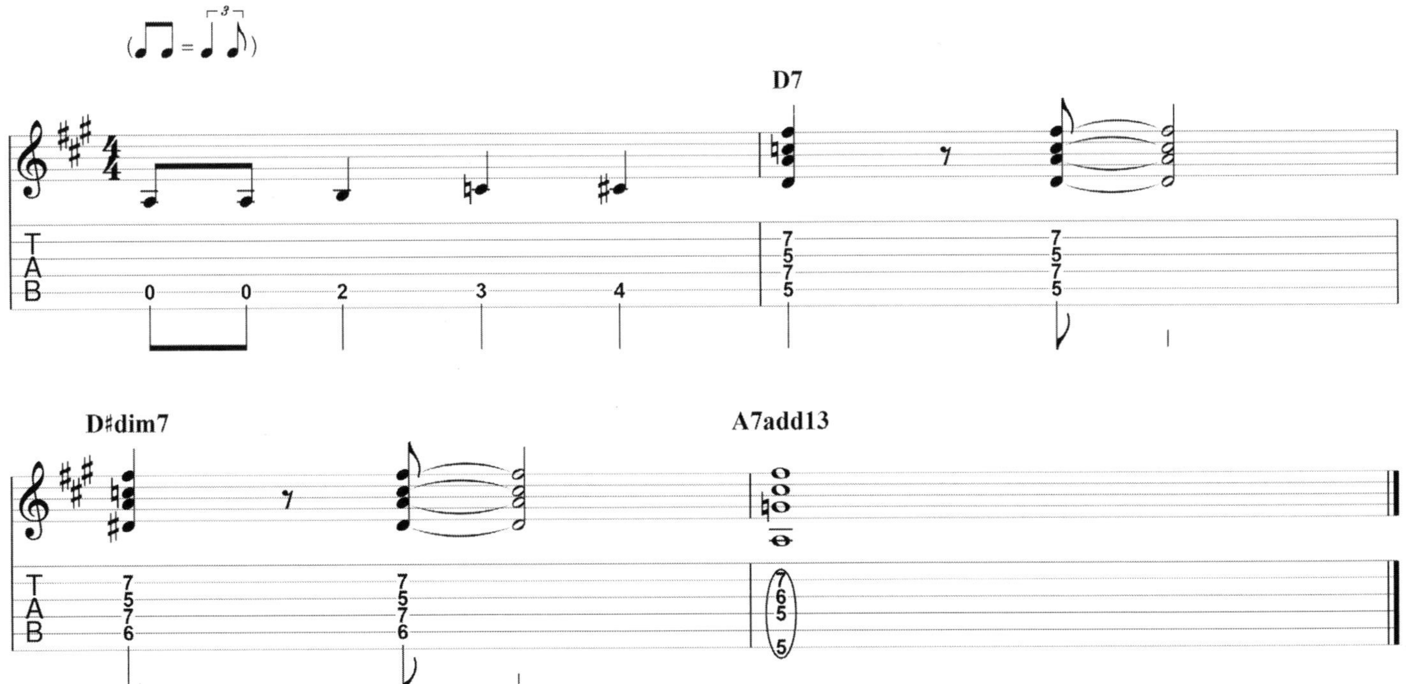

Another typical application happens over a ii-V turnaround, where the V chord is treated as an altered chord. You pretty much have free reign over how much of the measure of V you can alter; it's up to your imagination and your audience's tolerance. Diminished, augmented, and 7 sharp-9 chords all turn up the heat, which gets extinguished by arriving back home to the One (I) chord, as the 12-bar form begins again.

Listen to audio track 10 to hear three ii-V turnarounds in succession using examples of three different altered V chords —diminished, augmented and finally, the 7 sharp-9 chord known as "The Hendrix Chord"—each played within a 12-bar blues form.

Alt V Chords (Diminished, Augmented, 7♯9)

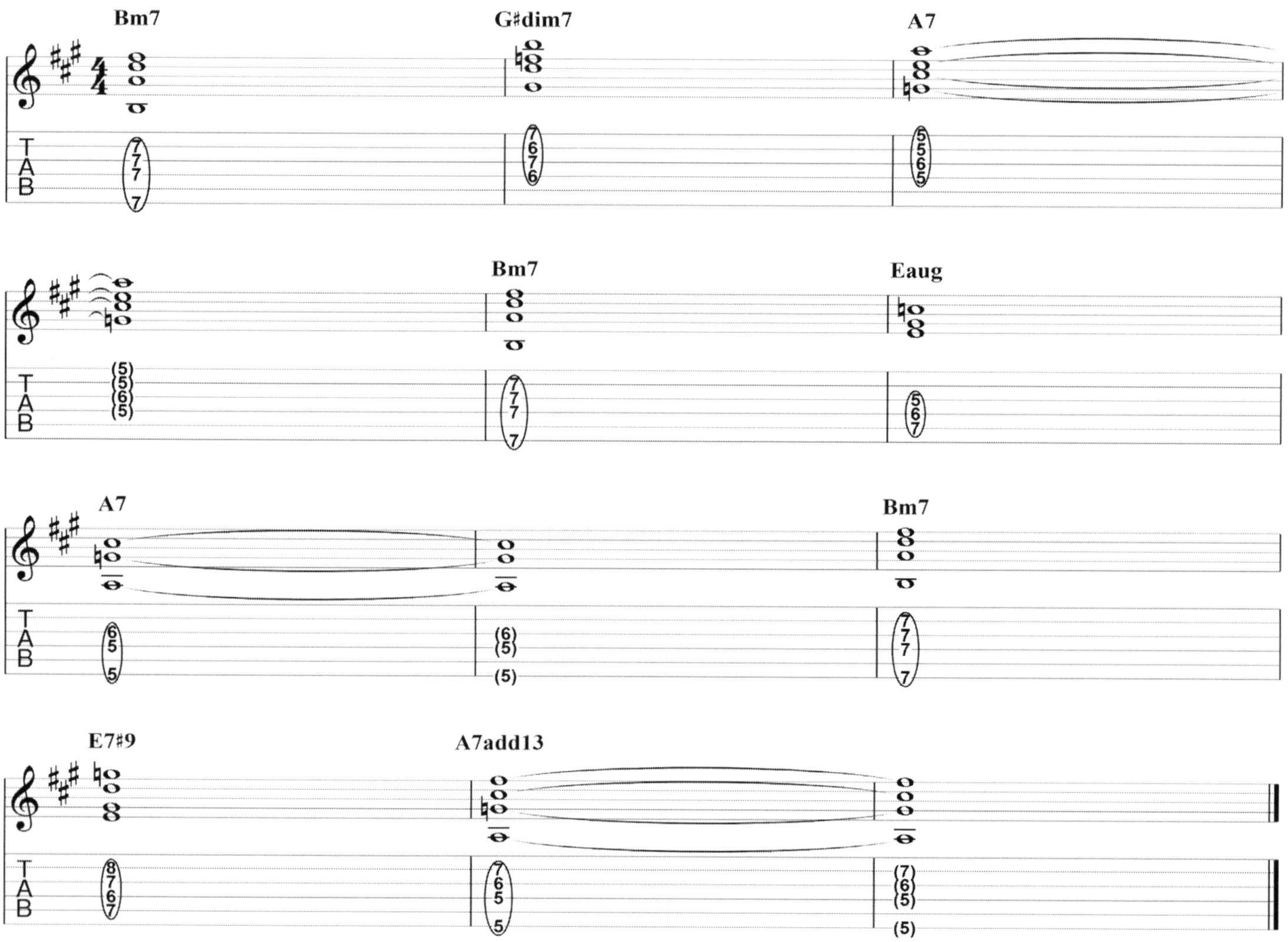

Bm7 G♯dim7 A7

Bm7 Eaug

A7 Bm7

E7♯9 A7add13

Essential Roots Guitar Rhythms

Next up, let's move into **Essential Roots Guitar Rhythms** and nail down specific rhythmic applications of these and other chord ideas.

The Beloved Shuffle and the Right Way to Play It

One of the backbones of roots style rhythm guitar is the shuffle. It is played with a dotted eighth-note feel. It's a partial chord figure with movement back and forth inside the chord against a steady bottom (root) note. (The same left-hand fingering can also be used to great effect with a straight eighth-note feel.) The shuffle is a killer, driving rhythm guitar technique that is essential in any type of roots guitar music. Whether using a shuffle (long-short triplet feel) or a straight-8 feel, make sure to emphasize the beats of each bar with your right hand: one and two and three and four and.

The most basic version of a shuffle rhythm pattern (and the one I use the most) relies on the two bottom strings of an open chord shape, with a varying note on the uppermost string against a constantly repeating lower root note. For example, to play a proper shuffle in the key of A, use an open A chord, and reduce it down to the root (open A string) and the fifth (the E note on the second fret of the D string). We are only using those two strings of the chord, so you want to focus both your left and right-hand fingers on this basic, partial chord.

For the first beat, play A and E together as an eighth note with a solid downstroke with your right hand. The next 8th note (on the and of beat 1) is only the root note (open A string) played with a solid right-hand downstroke. Next, we'll play the open A string together with an F-sharp on the D string, again played with a solid downstroke of the right hand. Follow that with only the root note (open A) played with a solid downstroke of the right hand.

We've built a pattern that alternates a 2-note interval or diad with a steady, pounding root note on the and of every beat in this sequence: root/5th interval, single root note, root/6th interval, followed by a single root note— and so on.

It's critical to isolate only the two bottom notes of the chord, or the single root note —with both hands in unison. It's also critical to develop the right-hand technique of playing this pattern with all downstrokes. You can use an alternate (up/down) right-hand strumming pattern, but to me it doesn't have the same rhythmic propulsion and authenticity that I hear in all those great Texas and Chicago blues records.

Note that the alternating bass note in the IV chord (in the key of A, that would be the open-D string) could also be further varied by adding a root/flat-7 interval as follows: root/5, root, root/6, root, root/flat-7, root, root/6, root, root/5 etc.

Using this system in the key of A, it's easily adaptable to play an entire 12-bar form with the basic shuffle pattern. To progress to the IV chord in a 12-bar form, shift to a partial open–D chord and use the two bottom strings exclusively to repeat the same pattern. Then as you progress through a 12-bar form, to make the V chord (E) happen, simply shift to the two bottom strings of an open-E chord and apply the same basic shuffle pattern.

For my money, Jimmie Vaughan and Billy F. Gibbons are the kings of this stuff. Stevie Ray Vaughan could also rock a Texas shuffle of the highest order. They are not the inventors of this style, as Jimmy Reed/Eddie Taylor and Chuck Berry were closer to the origins of the technique in terms of modern blues guitarists. Do your homework and check out the shuffle forefathers!

As mentioned earlier, this system also works great for a straight-eighth "chunka-chunka" feel—think "Johnny B. Goode" or "Roll Over Beethoven". Simply adjust the rhythm pattern in your right hand. Everything you played in your left hand pretty much stays the same.

The whole thing can be shifted to any key by re-fingering as a partial E or A form barré chord using the first finger of your left hand to play the root note, the ring finger of the left hand to hold the fifth of the chord, and the 4th finger to add the 6th and flat-7th on top, just as you played it in open position. See the next page for tab, notation and audio examples.

Listen to audio track 11 and play along with the open-position I-IV-V shuffle.

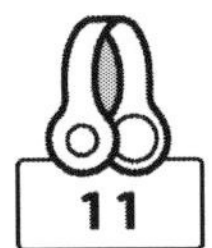

Open Position 12-Bar Shuffle in "A"

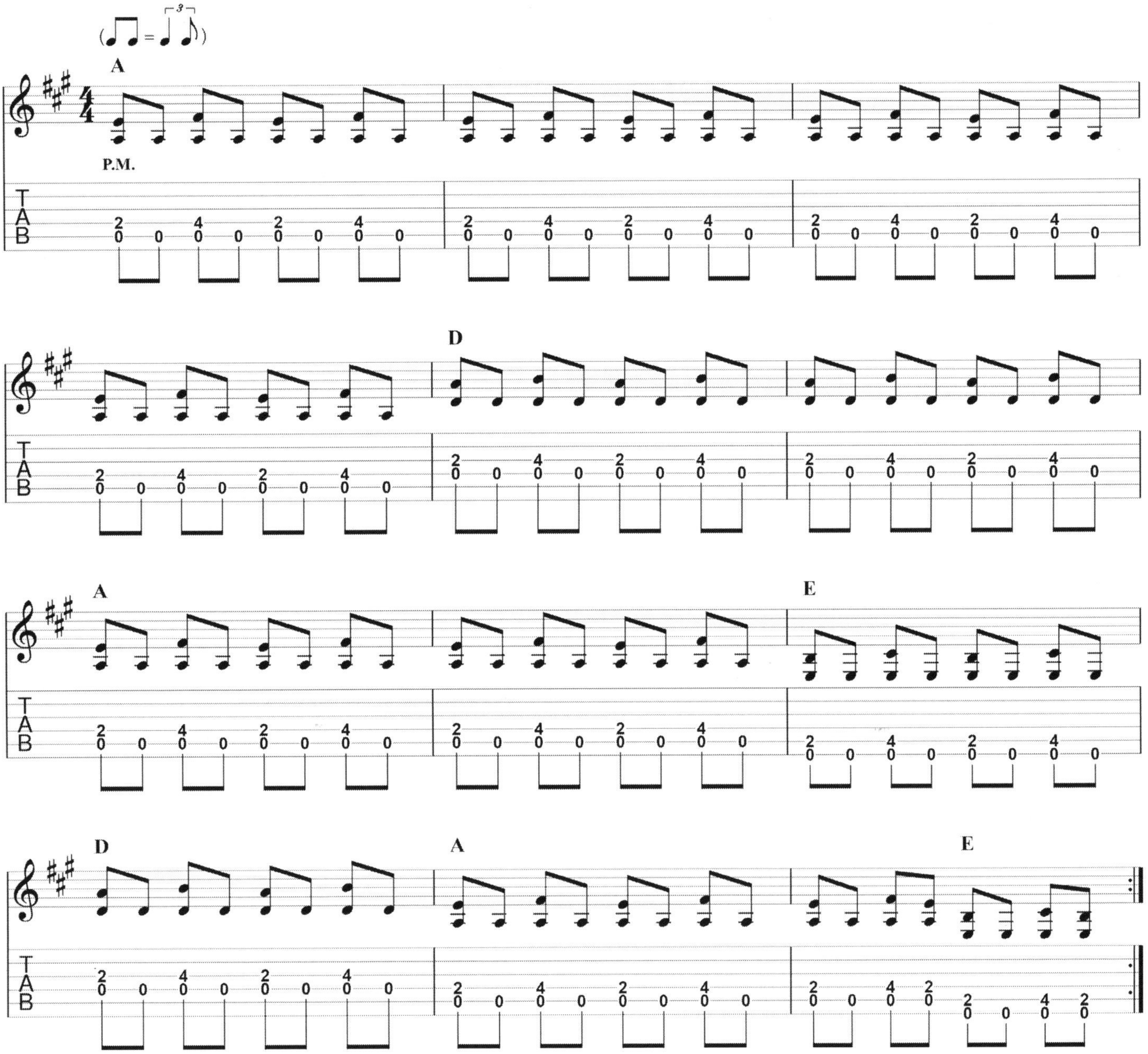

A

P.M.

D

A

E

D

A

E

Listen to audio track 12 and play along with the open-position I-IV-V straight-eighths rhythm in A.

Open Position 12-Bar Straight-Eighths in "A"

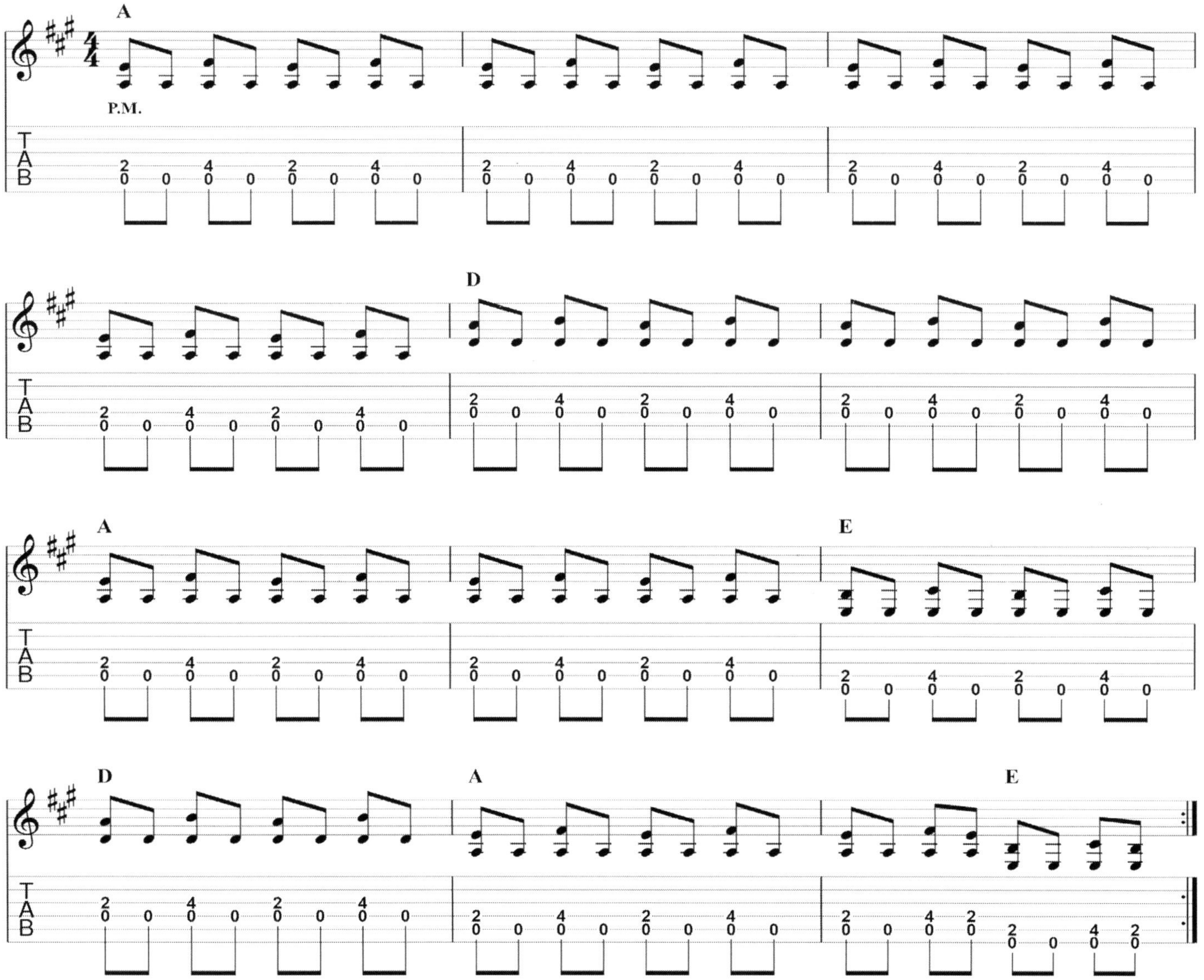

A

P.M.

D

A

E

D

A

E

Listen to audio track 13 and play along with the I-IV-V barré chord shuffle rhythm in A.

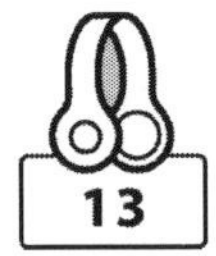

Barré Chord 12-Bar Shuffle in "A"

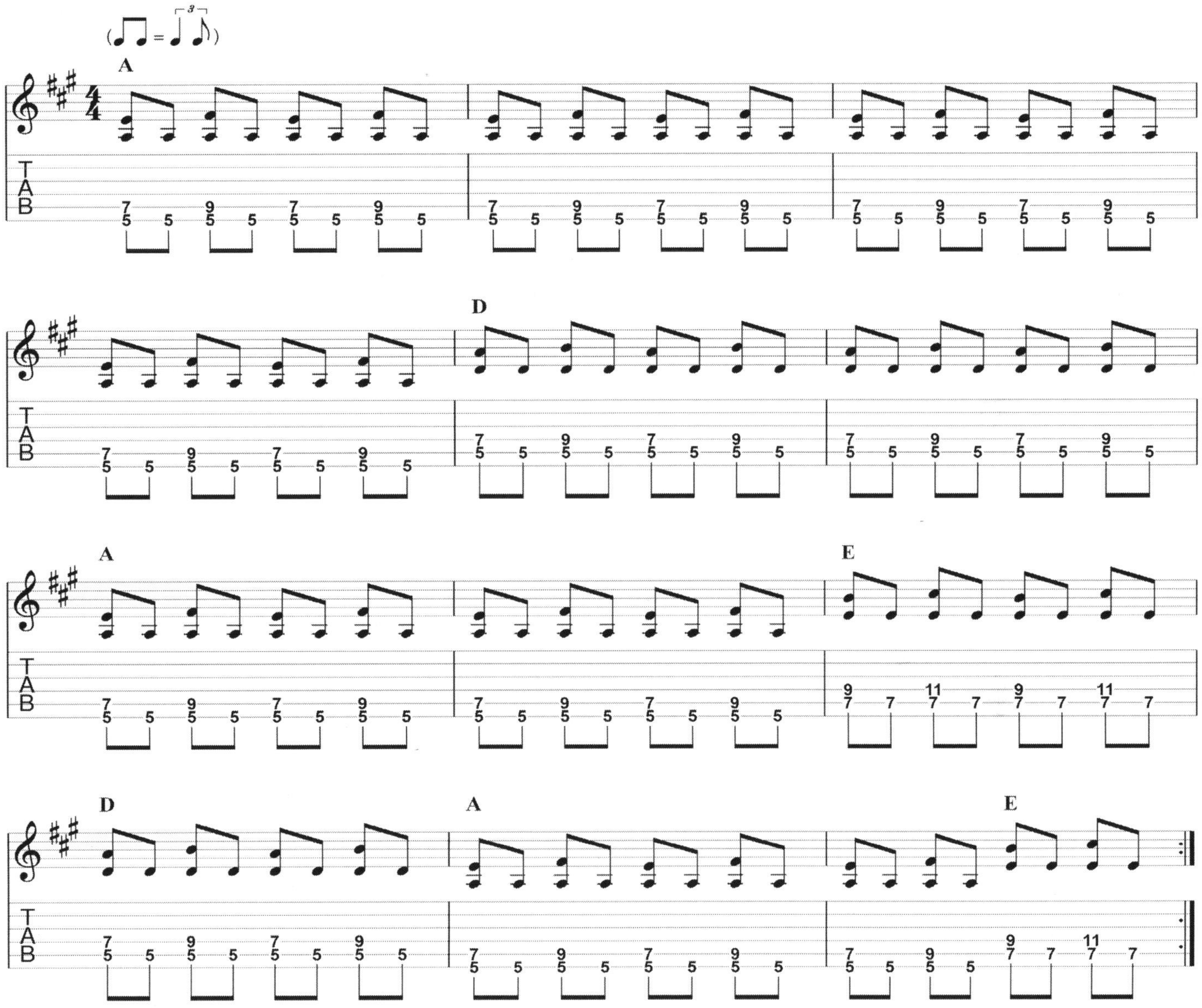

Listen to audio track 14 and play along with the I-IV-V barré-chord, straight-eighths rhythm in A.

Barré Chord 12-Bar Straight-Eighths in "A"

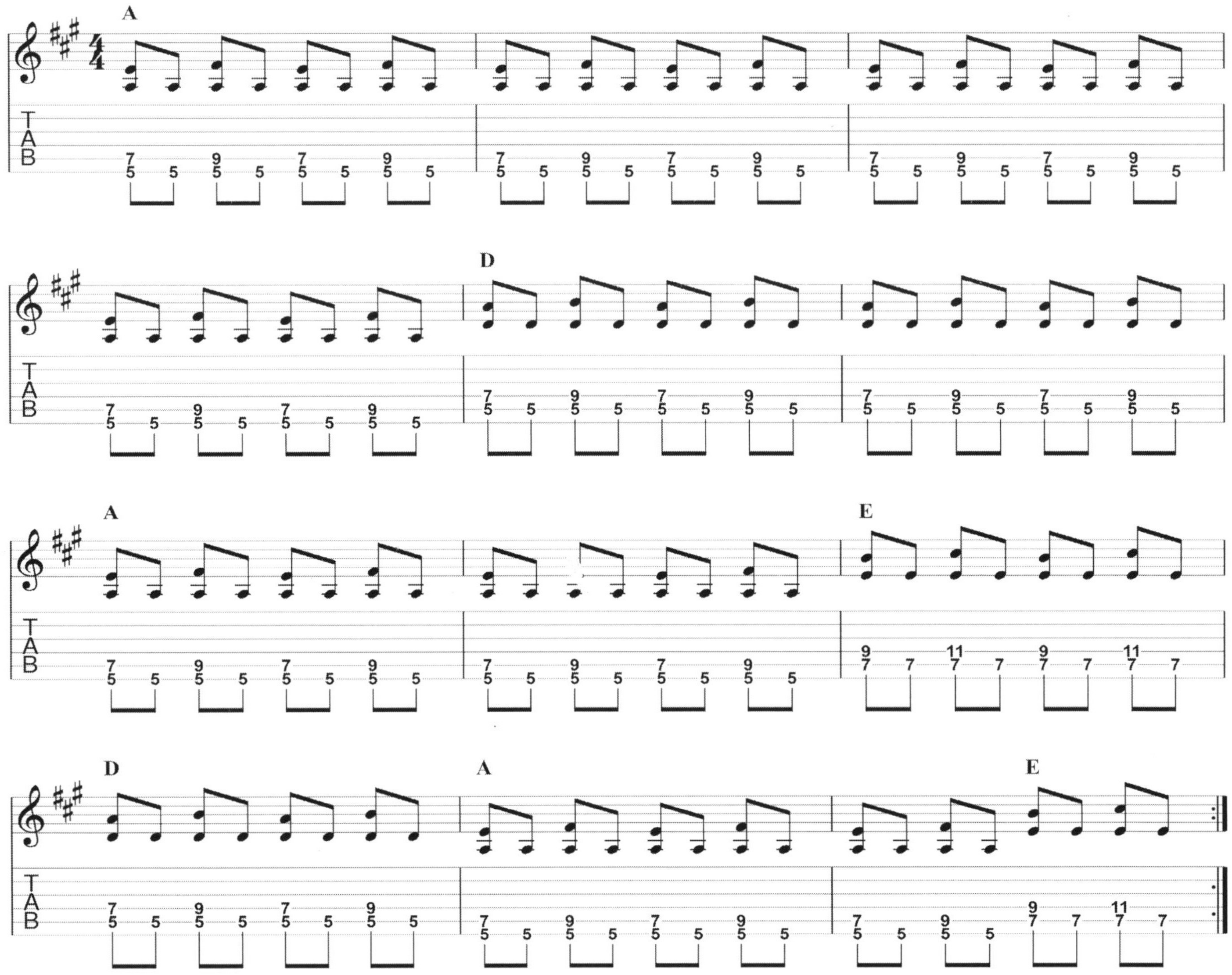

This page has been left blank to avoid an awkward page turn.

The Stevie Ray Vaughan (SRV) Shuffle Rhythm Variation

Absolutely worth mentioning, though a bit more complex—is the SRV (Stevie Ray Vaughan) shuffle. This variation of a shuffle rhythm uses the same basic concept of concentrating on the bottom portion of the chord. Here, however, an alternate down/up right-hand strumming pattern gives it a nice greasy swing feel.

Let's look at playing this one in E major. We are adding a third string (the D string) to the partial chord to flesh it out a bit more. We'll play the partial E chord with only the first finger of the left hand, playing the A and D strings at the second fret with a double stop (one finger pressing two notes in parallel) above the open E root, totaling 3 strings. This will be the basic chord shape throughout this shuffle. An alternate strumming pattern (down/up) is maintained by the right hand on each beat throughout the pattern.

We start with a right-hand downstroke, followed by an alternately strummed right-hand upstroke. The next two notes are both played on the low E string —a flat-third, G, as a downstroke, and a natural 3rd, G-sharp, as an upstroke. The next beat is a downstroke of all 3 bottom strings (open low E and the partial E chord, using a double stop of the A and D strings at the second fret) and an upstroke of the same 3 strings. This is followed with a downstroke on the low open-E string, and the C-sharp at the 4th fret of the A string, and then an upstroke of the partial E chord (E-B-E) on the bottom 3 strings.

This system can then be applied to a partial open-A chord (A-E-A) utilizing the bottom 3 strings of that chord. To make the turnaround B chord happen, use an A-form basic barré chord at the 2nd and 4th frets utilizing the A, D and G strings and slide up to the 5th and 6th frets with the left-hand ring finger to reach the flat-3rd and natural 3rd of the B turnaround chord, and progress backward through the partial A chord, before finally resolving to the E chord.

Note that the 3-note chords (E-B-E) and (A-E-A) do not contain the important 3rd degree of the scale which defines major chords from minor chords; consequently, these **power chords** can be used as substitutions for either the tonic major or tonic minor chord.

Listen to audio track 15, a 12-bar SRV shuffle in E, open position.

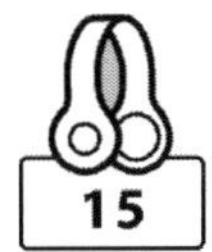

SRV Shuffle in Open "E"

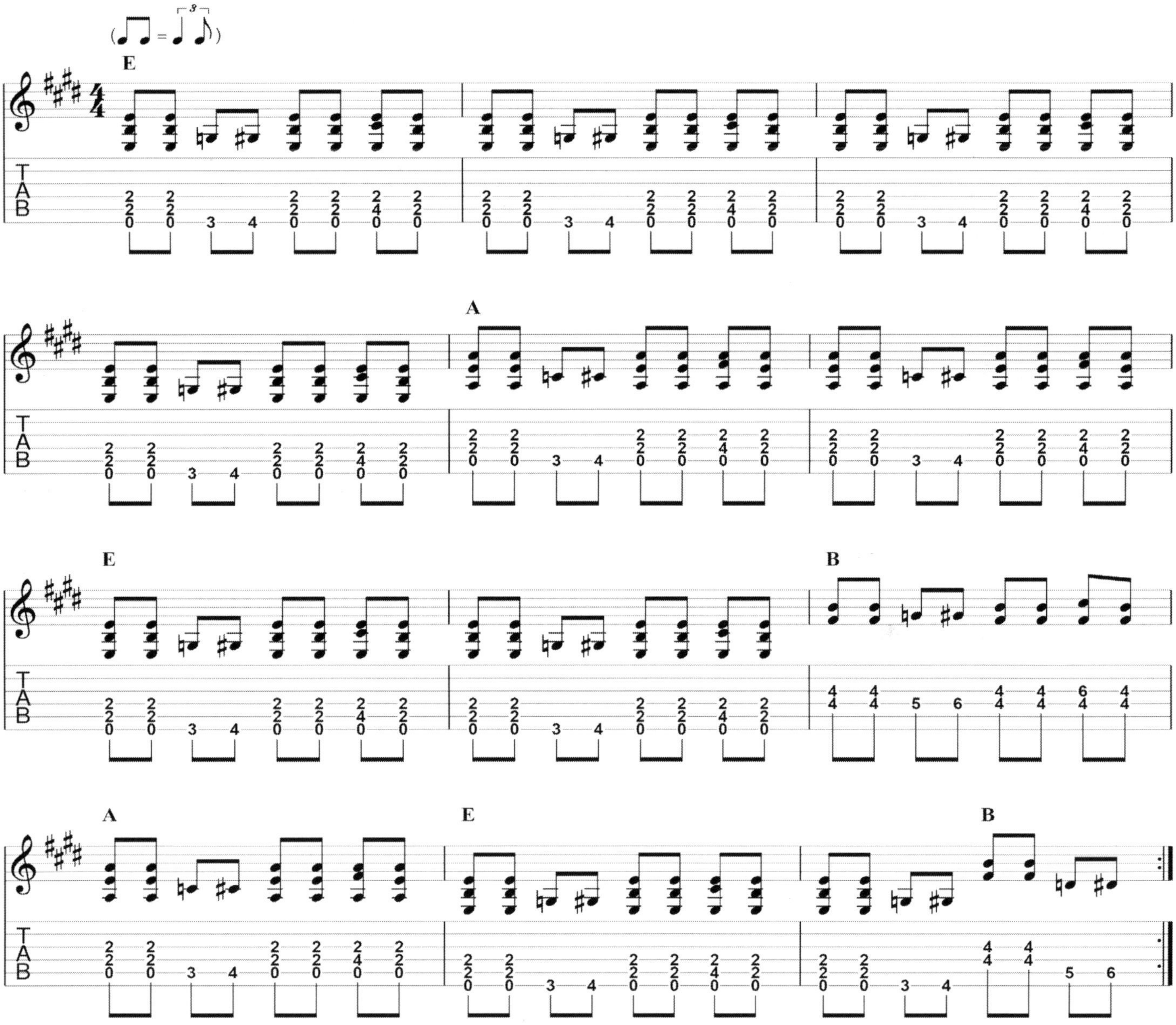

Rhythmic Placement
UPs and Charleston Rhythm Figures

UPs - Some guys call it the flat-tire beat. Only the weak second halves of each beat are accented here, and they syncopate in a hypnotic fashion with the steady groove of a shuffling rhythm section. They are typically played with upstrokes of the right hand. UPs are played four-to-the-bar. They are counted as "one **AND** two **AND** three **AND** four **AND**", with the numbers (one, two, etc.) being silent downbeats or rests, while the guitar strums happen on the **"ANDs"**, or upstrokes. It takes a bit of practice to master it, but UPs are a cool groove to play once you get it in your pocket. Any of the above-mentioned voicing examples will work with an UPs rhythmic pattern.

Try practicing this rhythm with play-along tracks 25, 26 or 43, where you can hear this rhythm guitar example applied.

Jump Blues UPs

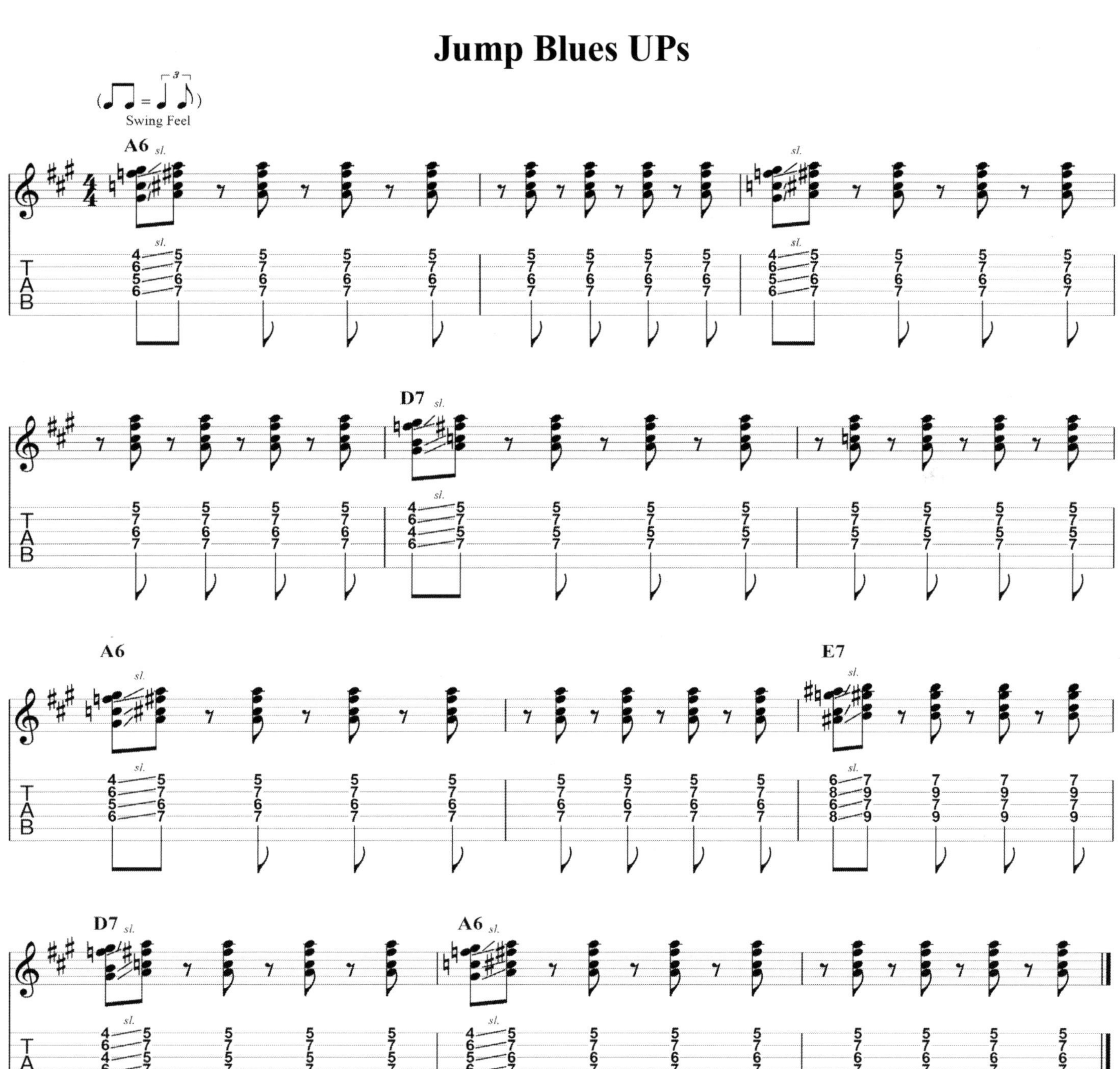

The Charleston Beat

Based on a dance craze from the 1920s of the same name, the Charleston is a different rhythmic figure for guitar that falls on the down beat of the One, followed by the AND of two ("ONE and two AND three and four and"). Along with a standard shuffle rhythm and UPs, the Charleston beat is a critical rhythm in your jump blues armament.

Practice this rhythm with play-along tracks 25, 26, or 43, where you can hear this rhythm guitar example applied.

The Allman Brothers used this rhythmic figure at the beginning of their arrangement of Elmore James' "Must Have Done Somebody Wrong" on the seminal "Live at The Fillmore" album. The whole rhythm section stomps the living daylights out of this beat through the entire intro of the song; 9th chords sound especially slick and genre-appropriate. When this rhythm is applied, it's played like this:

Jump Blues Charleston

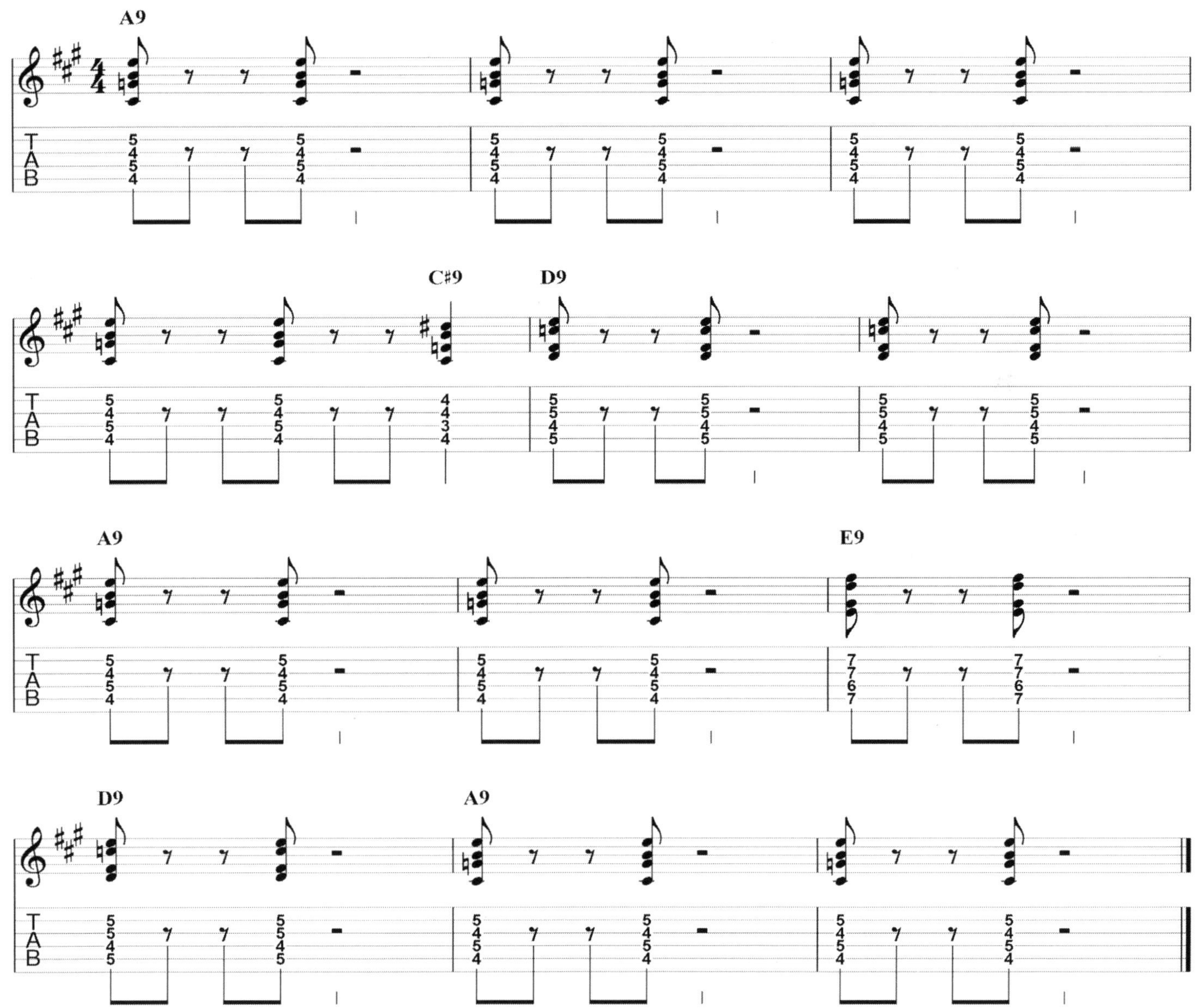

Orchestration for Guitars

All of the aforementioned partial-chord rhythm figures can be mixed and matched, providing wonderfully syncopated tapestries to weave on top of roots-style rhythm section grooves. Any two of the three different rhythmic patterns will combine nicely. Here are a couple of guidelines to apply so that you can really lock these rhythm figures in when combining them:

Playing in Different Registers by Stacking Voicings/Using the CAGED System as a Resource

A primary goal in orchestrating multiple guitar parts is to separate the positions of the voicings. Different inversions and chord shapes separate voicing by design, but it's also a great chance to break the habit of thinking of the key of G only being at the 3rd fret, or the key of A only being at the 5th fret. Every key is everywhere on the fretboard!

The most obvious example would be to combine Example 1 with Example 2 from the partial chord voicing examples in Chapter 2, as they both utilize 6th and 7th chords, but don't be afraid to try 9th or partial 9th chords, or 13th chords against 7th chords. Experiment and have fun finding interesting combinations. Don't forget that 7th, 9th and 13th chords all share common chord tones. Any two of these voicings can work together when weaving a cool two-guitar blend on top of a swinging rhythm section. It's exciting to discover which combinations work best in different sub-genres of roots or blues styles.

The CAGED system is based on the open chord shapes C, A, G, E, and D. By changing their fingerings into movable barré chord shapes, two guitarists could play different inversions of say, an A chord for example, in different positions which would yield different tonalities. A great strategy is to use partial versions of those different voicings as well, perhaps one guitar focusing on the lower (E, A & D strings), while a second guitar might focus on the higher (G, B and E) strings.

Accurate rhythmic placement and execution are critical. You've worked hard to figure out these different rhythm guitar ideas so that you can pump some fresh blood into your sound. Don't blow all that hard work with sloppy execution.

Utilizing Different Tonal Variations

When layering two guitars over a rhythm section, try to create contrasting sounds with the two instruments; maybe set one guitar with more treble from the bridge pickup, and the other guitar with a fatter sound from the neck pickup, or one guitar with a cleaner sound and one with a warmer tone—rolled back, or slightly overdriven. You may want to try some reverb on one guitar—an effect that will typically work best with a sparse rhythm pattern— and run the other guitar dry. One instrument might use a *Leslie* effect. Be careful about having everybody running effects at once; you don't want it to sound like cats in a blender.

In the next chapter, we'll look at some soloing concepts you might not have considered before. A few of the things we looked at in the **Rhythm Guitar Concepts** chapter will carry over into the way we approach soloing in different roots styles.

CHAPTER 3: SOLOING CONCEPTS

Chord Tones and Soloing Reference Points

Probably 99% of guitarists playing the blues or different related roots styles utilize the good old pentatonic scale; we always have, and we always will. The problem is, there are only so many ways to "climb up and down the ladder". That said, the pentatonic scale works so darn well with the blues, rockabilly and other styles that it would be a mistake to throw it out completely. So, we're going to rev it up with some extra scale and chord tones.

Remember how we talked about adding or emphasizing chord and scale tones in partial chords? Emphasizing those same tones in soloing will yield phrases and licks that really make an impact. Since 6ths, 7ths, 9ths, and 13ths sound great in roots-style chords, it only makes sense that those same chord tones will help us to create lines that sound more hip or modern. First, let's illustrate **The Box, or pentatonic scale**— for those of us who already use it but don't have an actual name for it.

Listen to audio track 16 for the 5th fret pentatonic scale in A minor/C major.

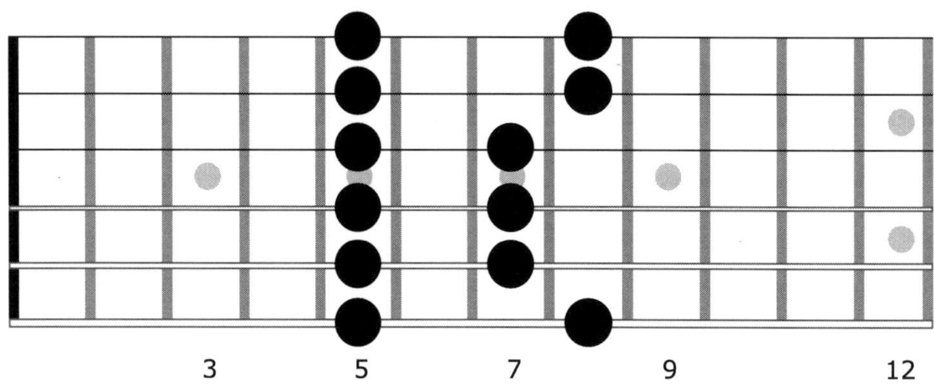

A Minor / C Major Pentatonic Scales

Pattern 1

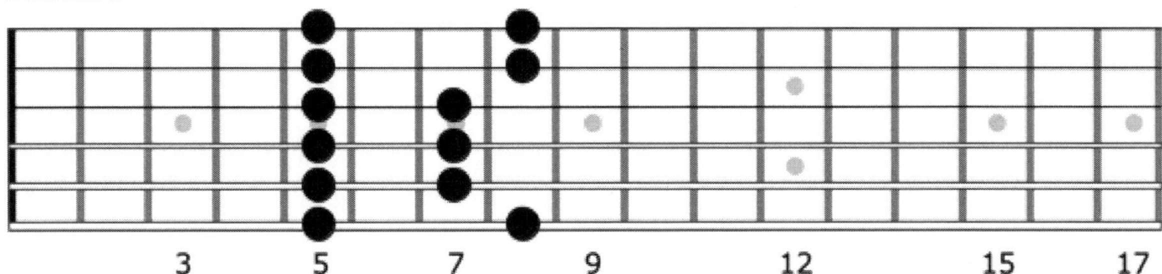

Pattern 2

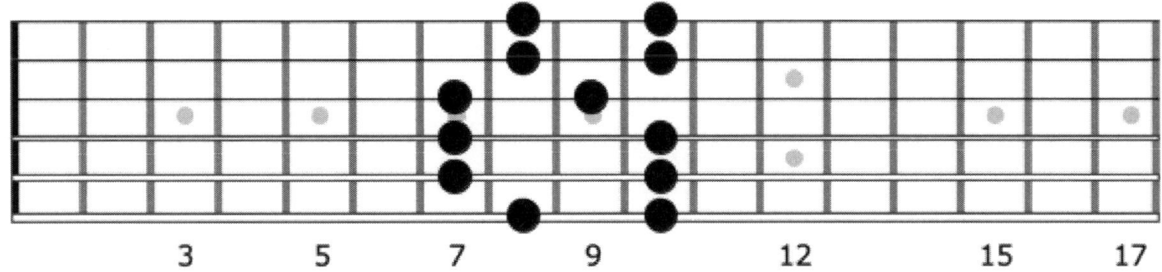

Pattern 3

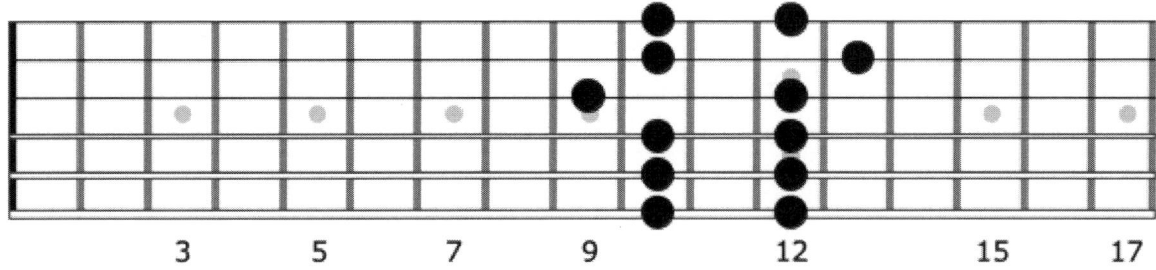

Pattern 4

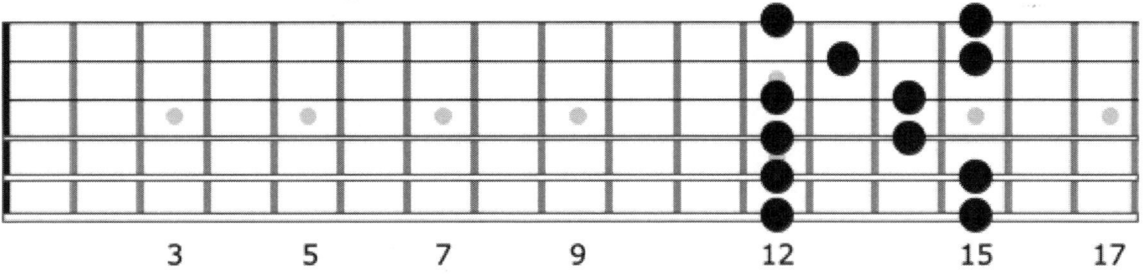

Pattern 5

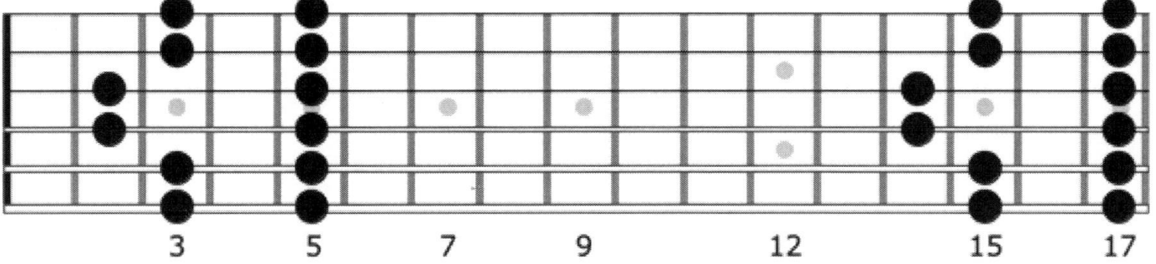

Just like the relative major and minor 7-tone + octave scales, the relative major and minor pentatonic scales are made up of exactly the same notes; you just have to start from or focus on the right "tonic" or first note.

The first pattern above, with the first finger placed at the fifth fret of each string— is one of the easiest pentatonic patterns to memorize. In addition, on strings 1 and 6, you have the minor tonic (A) under your first finger, and the major tonic (C) under your 4th finger, providing a handy guide to the desired key. This seems to be the first "box" or pattern that everyone learns, so we'll call it "Pattern #1". There are four more pentatonic boxes as shown above.

Note that all pentatonic patterns have only 2 notes per string. This is because we are eliminating the half tones that distinguish major from minor scales and substituting intervals of a tone-and-a-half. This absence of half tones allows us to play the same pentatonic patterns over the chords in a major or its relative minor key.

Note that wherever fingers 1 and 3 play a whole-tone interval (2 frets apart) you can comfortably add the middle or "passing" tone to your scale. To avoid predictability, don't add the passing tone every chance you get; mix it up instead.

Notice that the **natural halftones**, E-F and B-C are missing from both the A minor pentatonic and the "relative" C major pentatonic scales; neither has the B or F notes. It is the position of the half tones that defines whether it's a pure minor or major scale; those half tones lie between grades 2-3 and 5-6 for minor, and between 3-4 and 7-8 for major. With no sharps or flats, the actual notes of the two scales are identical, so the same pentatonic scale pattern will fit tunes in either A minor or C major; it's only the choice of the **tonic** or first note of the scale that determines the scale's function and identity.

Notice that in our fretting hand, we have a convenient guide to the minor and major tonic notes within **The Box.** On strings 1 and 6 in first position, the minor tonic, A lies under your first finger, and 3 frets higher, the major tonic, C lies under your 4th finger. How cool is that!

Here's an important note: the relationship between A minor and C major exists between any two chords a minor 3rd (3 frets) apart: Em to G; F-sharp minor to A; B minor to D, and so forth. The entire pentatonic template shifts based on a given key or tonal center of a song. Experiment and explore the fretboard to acclimate yourself.

It's also good practice to scat sing along with your pentatonic licks and riffs; it's great ear training and will help you to gradually anticipate note locations and ultimately give you creative ideas for soloing phrases.

Focusing on the A minor pentatonic scale, check out some ideas of how we might move through several of the positions in a linear fashion (up and down the fretboard) as opposed to just climbing up and down each position separately. As you move up and down the fretboard, use fingers 1 and 3 to transition to other positions, and sprinkle in some passing/chromatic tones here and there. Try to avoid predictability in note choices.

Minor Pentatonic Linear Lick Across First 3 Positions

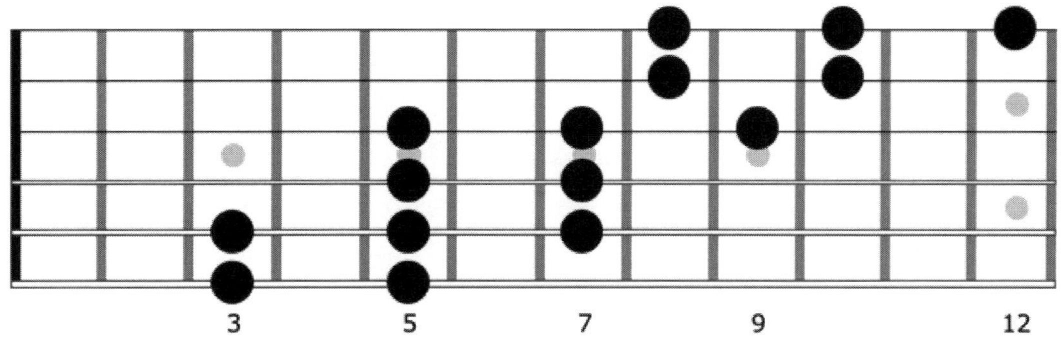

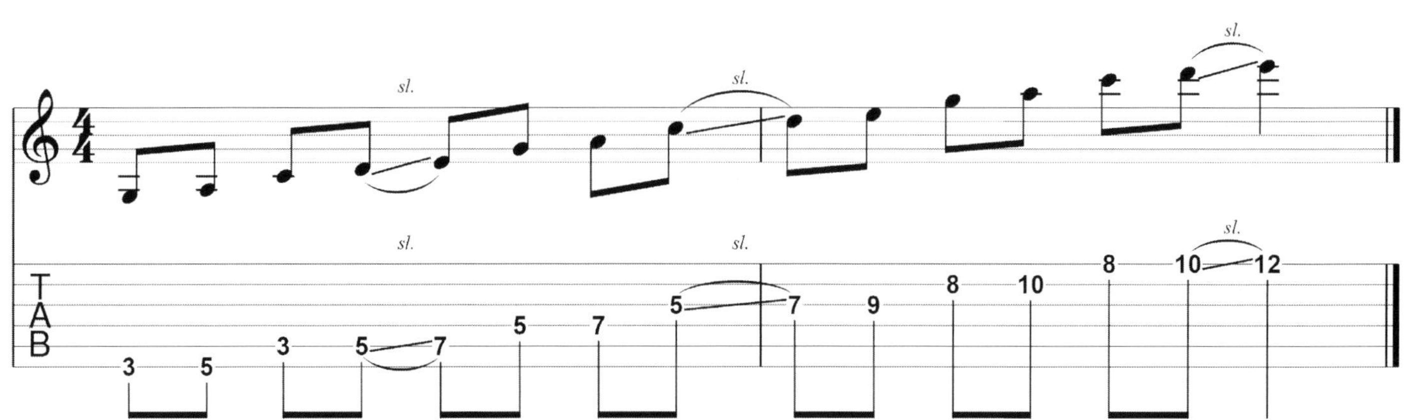

Our next soloing template continues to expand the pentatonic template. We'll add an extra note per string for a total of 3 notes on each string. We'll be including a major 2nd, a flat-5, a 6th, and a major 7th. Note that the flat-5 notes can be played by either pressing a string to a fret or by bending a note up a half tone from a lower fret.

Listen to audio track 17 to hear the Blues Scale with 3 notes per string.

The Blues Scale

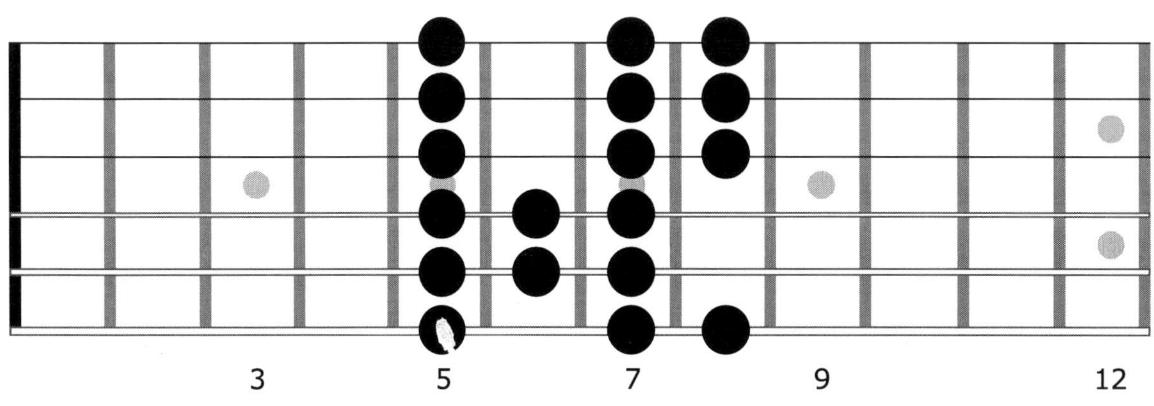

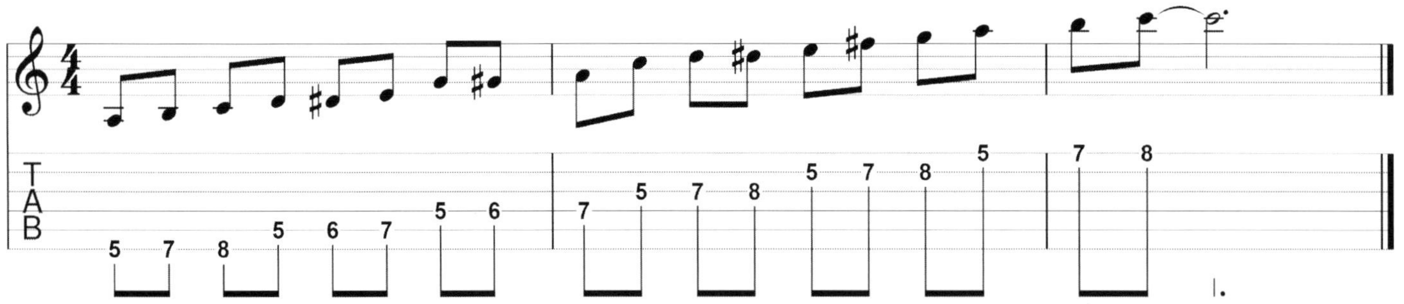

Still using the minor pentatonic box as a template, let's embellish the blues scale by adding more scale tones and chromatic **passing tones** that are not part of the original minor scale. We've added chromatic notes on the A, D and G strings.

Listen to audio track 18 to hear the Embellished Blues Scale with 3-4 notes per string.

Embellished Blues Scale

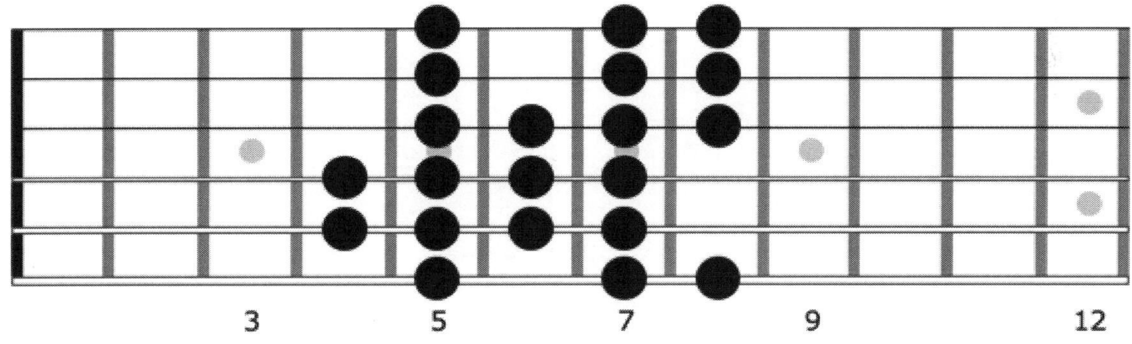

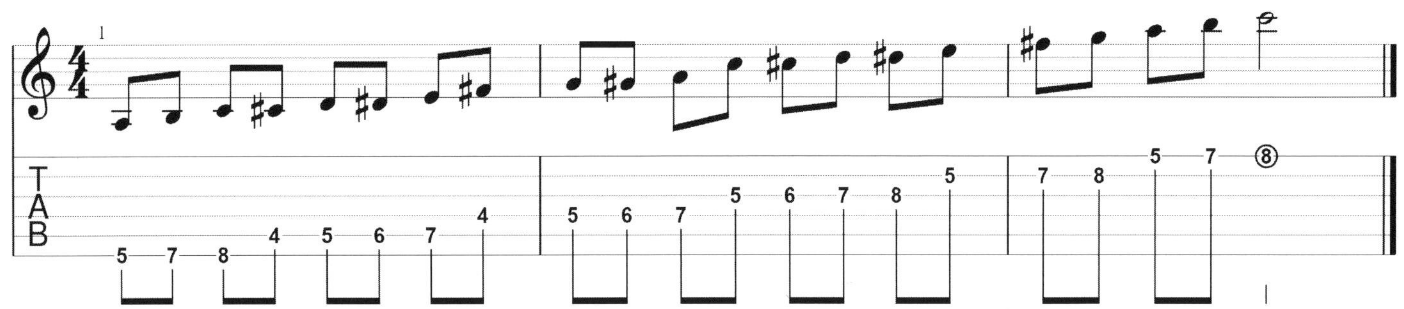

If we add just a few more tones from the chromatic and major scales to our pentatonic/blues scale template, then Holy Cow, we've got a TON of options. Again, with the A minor pentatonic pattern as its foundation, we now have a vaguely Mixolydian scale to explore.

Listen to audio track 19 to hear the Expanded-Mixolydian like scale with 3 to 5 notes per string.

Mixolydian/Nearly Chromatic Scale

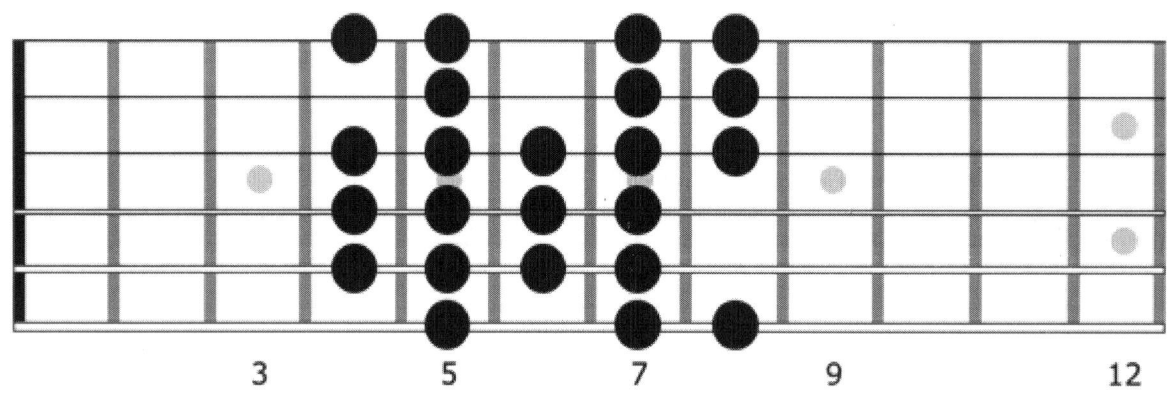

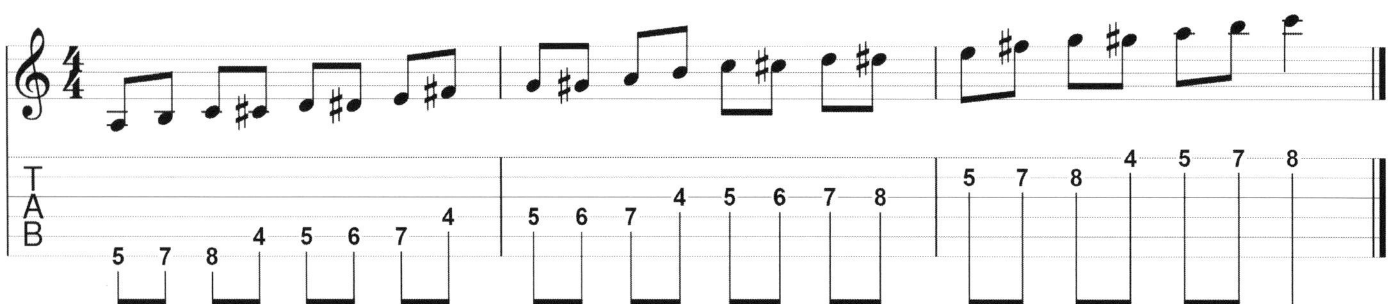

Strictly speaking, the A Mixolydian scale is based on the 5th note or degree of the D major scale which has two sharps, F♯ and C♯; you could also think of it as the A major scale with a flatted-7th, G-natural. Make friends with the extra 3rds, 6ths and 9ths that we have superimposed. Try to center your "Chi" over the good old pentatonic and visualize adding the 3rd, 6 th and 9th notes of the scale/chord. The corresponding 6th and 9th chords sound killer in the blues, and —guess what— those same scale tones bring exactly the same flavor!

Based on the C major scale with no sharps or flats, here are the common modal scales:

Ionian	C D E–F G A B–C	The major scale
Dorian	D E–F G A B–C D	Minor with a raised 6th
Phrygian	E–F G A B–C D E	Minor with a lowered 2nd
Lydian	F G A B–C D E–F	Major with a raised 4th
Mixolydian	G A B–C D E–F G	Major with a lowered 7th
Aeolian	A B–C D E–F G A	The pure minor scale
Locrian	B–C D E–F G A B	Rarely used

For ear training purposes, play each of these scales on a keyboard using only the white keys; sing along with the letter names or solfege syllables: Do—Re—Mi-Fa—Sol—La—Si (or Ti)-Do, taking note of where the natural half tones, Mi-Fa and Si-Do occur.

Avoiding "The Ones"

Briefly, there are two "Ones" we're trying to avoid – the tonic "One" and the first downbeat of the bar (as in ONE – two – three – four). While neither the root tonic "One", nor the first downbeat of the bar "One" would be considered "wrong", they are both textbook examples of predictability in terms of soloing. There are, no doubt, times when they are a great choice and I'm not suggesting we never use them, but if we take an honest look at our licks and phrases, we find that we use them most, if not all the time— to begin or end licks – or both!

They are so perfect and safe that we train ourselves to go there on autopilot to either begin or end phrases. Try to end a lick with a flatted third to a natural third or begin a phrase with the fifth instead of the One. What about a 6th or 7th? Chord tones are our friends. *(See the first four bars of the diagram labeled "T-Bone Style Lick" for example).*

Finally, don't forget to let your phrases breathe. Apply rests in between phrases and licks. Mohammad Ali was so dangerous because you couldn't tell when he was coming. Remember, rests are meant to be played. They are not just an absence of sound; they are tools. Utilize them!

In a similar fashion, try to start a phrase with the "and" (upbeat) of three, four, or two. Anticipate the approaching bar. T-Bone Walker, the patron saint of jump blues, spearheaded a style that is a perfect example of these variants (avoiding three Ones at once –Bravo!!). Check out the T-Bone style exercise on the upcoming page. The lick begins with the 5th of the scale and ends on the natural 3rd – and starts on the AND (upbeat) of beat three. It's only a 3- beat lick at the top, but it packs a ton of cool for only 3 thoughtfully placed beats. Note that the initial theme continues on through the entire head with modifications to fit the 12-bar form, a technique called "Thematic Soloing".

Thematic Soloing

Briefly, thematic soloing takes a catchy line or melody and recycles it, if you will, adapting the main content of the line and adjusting a chord tone or two to fit the additional chords of the song form. Typically used to great effect in the blues, some shining examples of this technique include "Jumping at the Woodside" and "One O'Clock Jump" by Count Basie, Thelonious Monk's "Blue Monk", and the 1957 toe-tapper "Little Bitty Pretty One" from Thurston Harris & The Sharps.

Listen to audio track 20 to hear a T-Bone Walker-style application of thematic soloing over a 12-bar blues track. You can also try this concept with play-along tracks 25, 26 or 43.

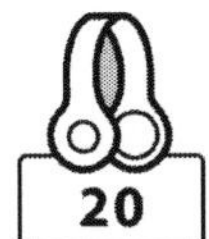

T-Bone-Style Lick

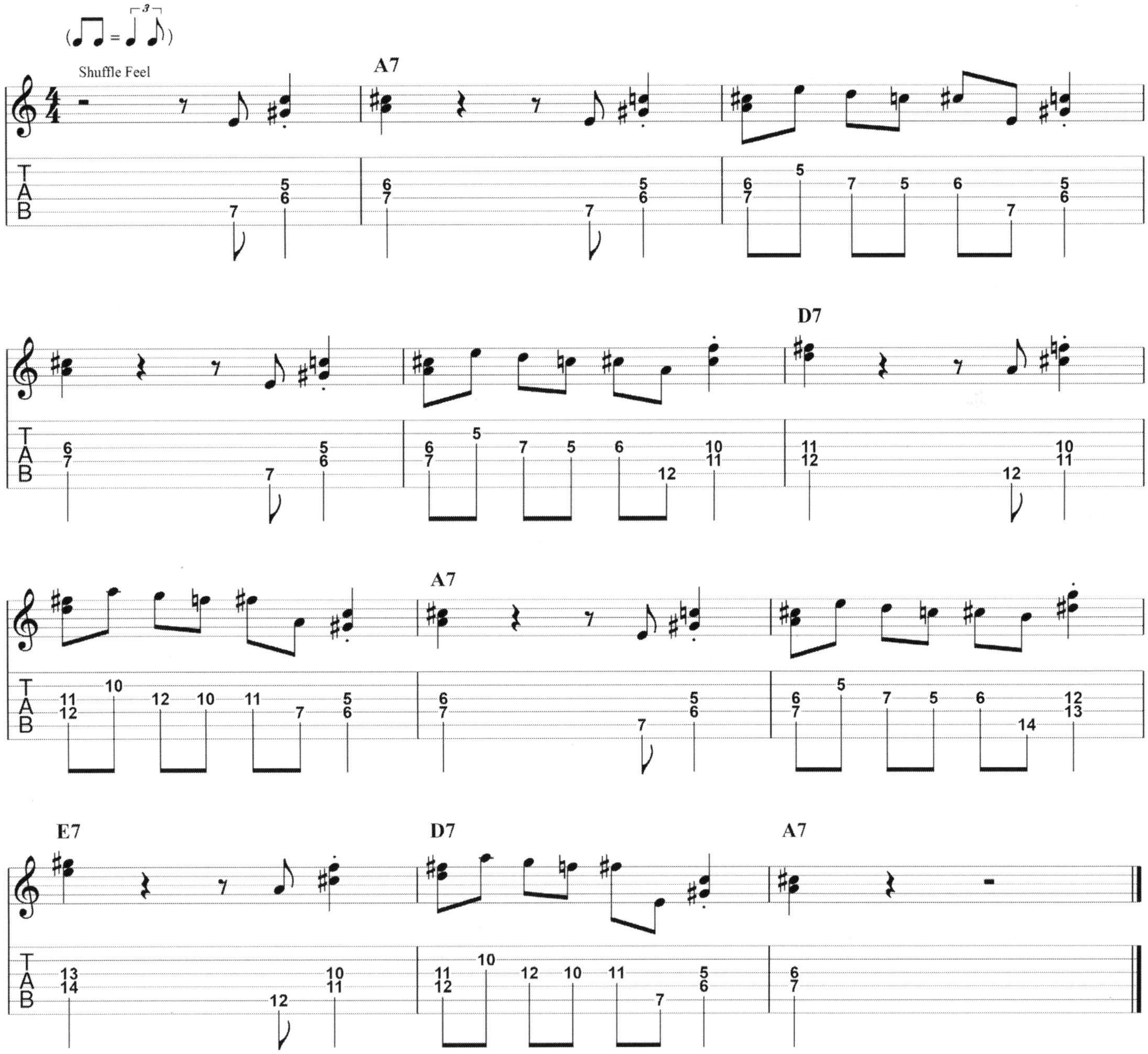

Shuffle Feel

A7 | D7 | A7 | E7 | D7 | A7

As another great example of avoiding the One AND thematic soloing, Buster Brown's killer 1960 R&B hit records gave birth to this horn inspired line. It sits perfectly atop a standard issue shuffle.

On the *first* bar of the figure, the rhythmic placement falls on the beat of 2, the **AND** of 2 and beat 3; then in the second bar it is played on the down beat 1, beat of 2, the **AND** of 2, and beat 3. It's usually played as a **2-bar figure**, but is here modified to fit a 12-bar form; remember, with the V and IV of a 12-bar form (bars 9 and 10) each only lasts a bar as seen below.

Listen to audio track 21 to hear another thematic soloing example played over a 12-bar blues track. You can try playing thematic soloing over play-along tracks, 25, 26 or 43.

Buster Brown-Style Lick

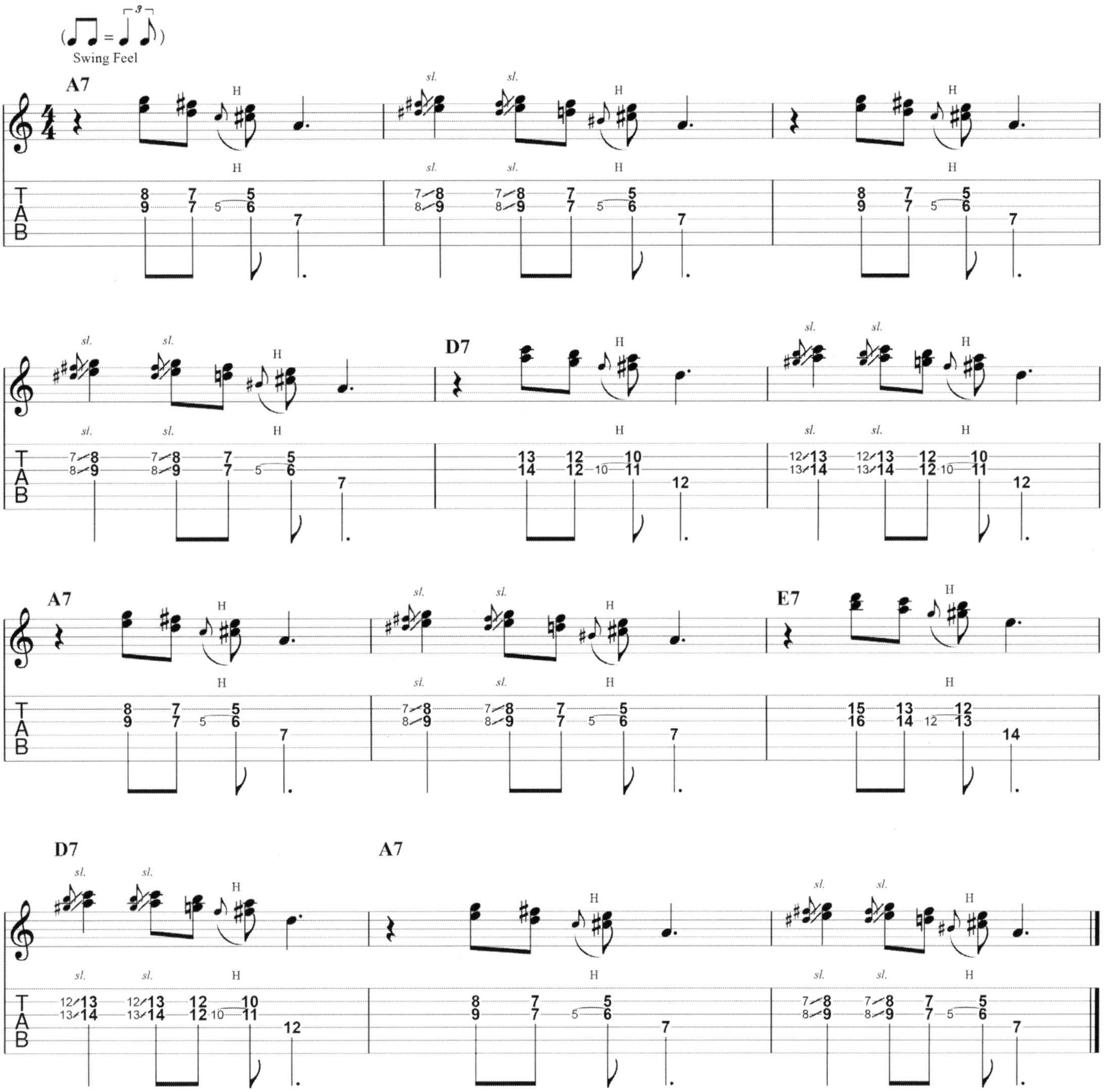

Swing Feel

A7 | | | | D7 | | A7 | | E7 | D7 | A7 |

Soloing Outside – Half-Step and Diminished Scales

Tension and Release

The practice of creating tension and releasing or resolving it at specific points in a musical structure is a tool that yields some really powerful results in your playing. There are small windows of one or two beats as you approach pending chord changes that allow you to temporarily create harmonic tension that transitions into the anticipated chord, which creates a sense of musical relief to the listener. These transitions create musical thrills for both our listeners and for us as performers. It takes some dedication to master these little windows as, depending on the tempo, the opportunities appear and evaporate quickly. They can be challenging to navigate – but the musical payoff is glorious when you get it under your belt!

This strategy works EXACTLY the same way in terms of the mechanics and the windows of opportunity discussed in the prior "grease" chords section, where we applied musical tension and subsequently resolved it.

In both half-step approaches and borrowing a beat from the previous/approaching bar, the processes are the same. Try to find interesting chord tones – 6, 7, 9, 13 etc. and build a 3 or 4-note arpeggio that you then drop on the last one or two beats of the bar a half-step below or above a "target" chord in the next measure.

Those Funny Arpeggios

Just like those "funny" Chords, if we're in A and the IV chord is D, apply a C♯7, C♯6 or C♯13 **lick or arpeggio** approaching our IV chord from a half step BELOW, OR use an E♭7, E♭6, or E♭13 **lick or arpeggio**, approaching our IV chord from a half step ABOVE. Approaching from either side works, and the release happens either way when we land on our target (IV) chord. Add a chord tone or two from the target chord for the final note of your phrase as you land on the chord. Slippin' and slidin'! See the following example of Half-Step Approaches on the next page.

Listen to audio track 22 for an example of half-step approaches to soloing over a 12-bar blues track with a ii-V turnaround. You can also try this technique over the ii-V turnaround using play-along audio tracks 41, 42, 44, 45, 47, and 48.

Half-Step and Diminished Approaches

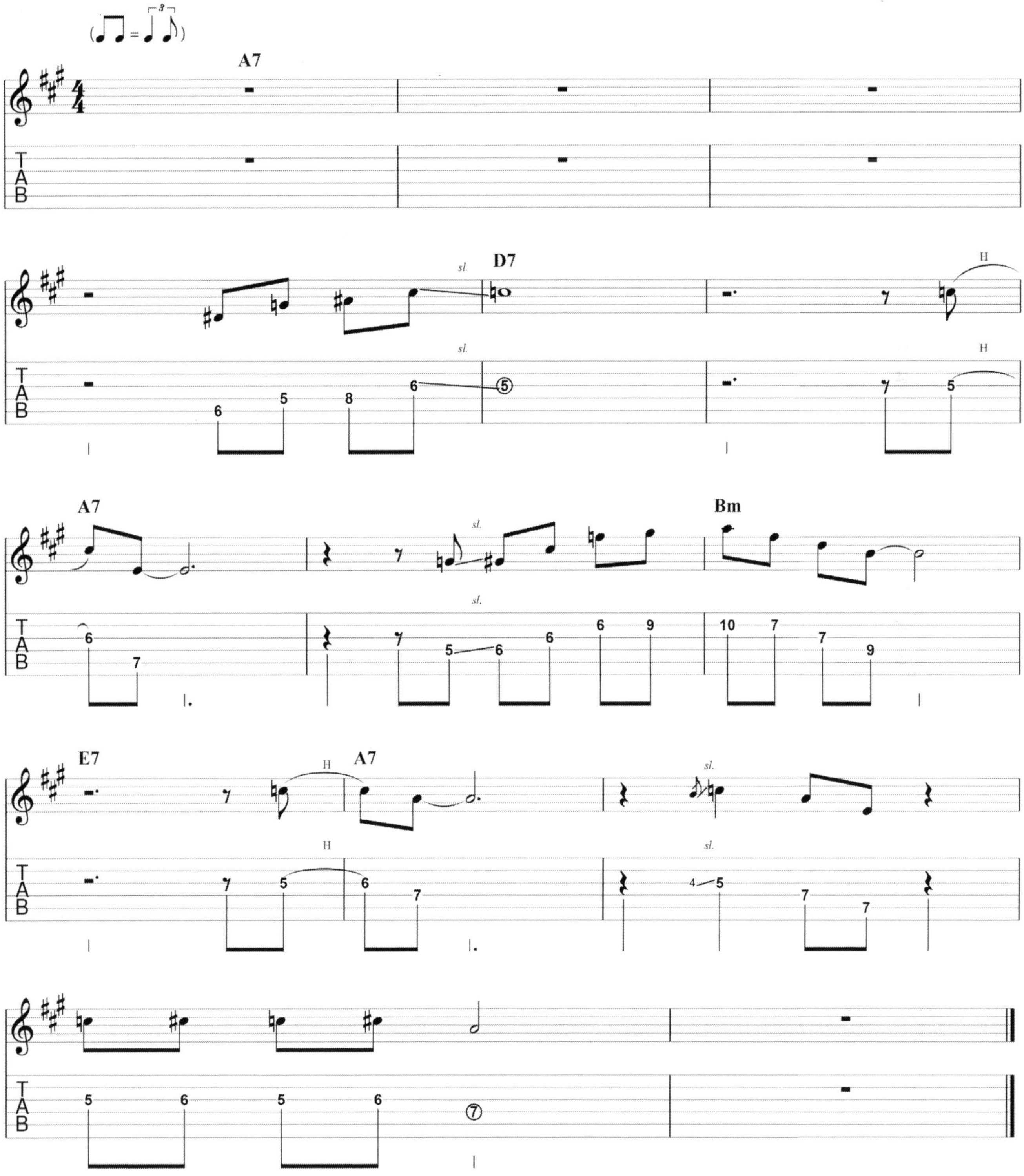

A7 D7 A7 Bm E7 A7

Theoretically, we can approach virtually ALL changes by applying the half-step and diminished approach. It would sound pretty odd to do it at every single chord change; it works on paper but try to use some common sense (a rare commodity for me!). Practice it at a slow tempo to get used to the process. T-Bone Walker's classic tune "Stormy Monday" is a great template for practicing these moves, as it is a slow blues – easier to navigate at slower tempos.

Diminishing Over the IV Chord

Here's another technique that we can borrow from the above "grease" chord section from the Rhythm Guitar Concepts chapter. Wherever a diminished chord can be placed to create tension, say, the last half of a section of IV, we can just as well utilize a diminished scale. In playing a 12-bar form in A, an easy way to create that sound would be to play a 4-note arpeggio of a D7 chord over bar 5 and then play the same 4 notes but raise the root to an E-flat, which would be E-flat-F-sharp-A-C over the 5th bar (the second bar of D). A simple arpeggio of four quarter notes over each bar illustrates the idea clearly. It may sound a bit basic played super straight but vary your rhythmic emphasis and see if you can make it swing. Think of the phrasing used by horn or keyboard players for inspiration.

Listen to audio track 23 to hear a basic diminished lick soloing example over the IV chord, resolving back to the I chord.

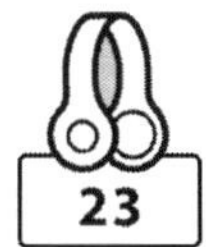

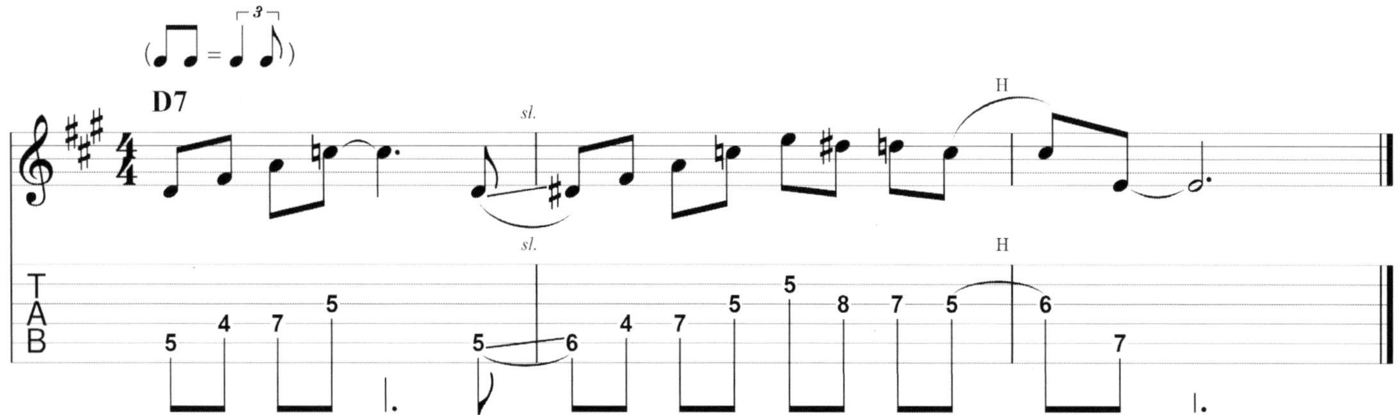

See the following 12-bar forms for practice in applying tension and release in "windows of opportunity" in your soloing.

Two Basic 12-Bar Forms with V-IV-I Turnarounds Using Half-Step "Grease" Chord Approaches

Use the last 1 or 2 beats of the bars as shown in **bold** to approach the next chord change from a half-step below or above to create tension/release.

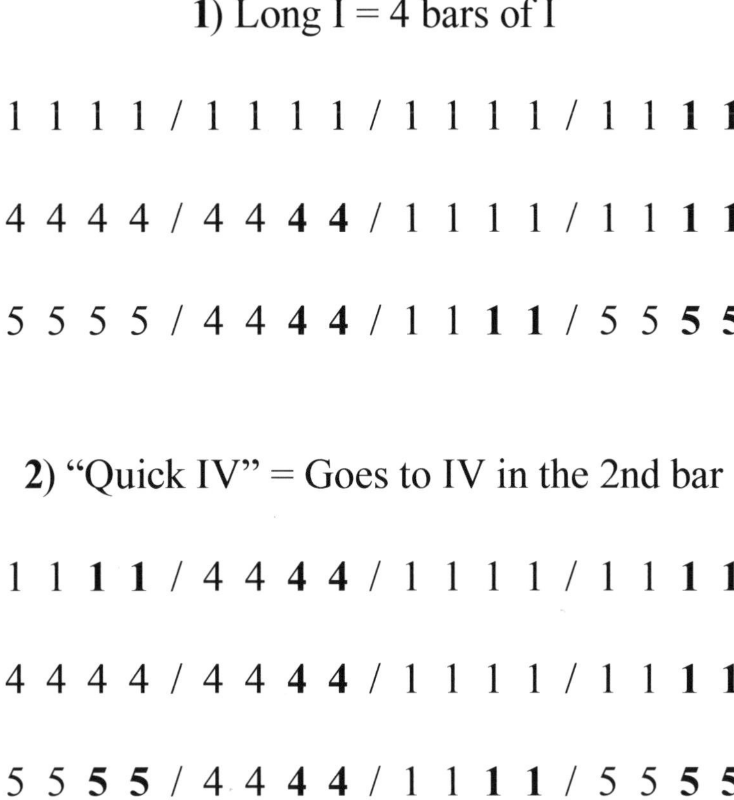

1) Long I = 4 bars of I

1 1 1 1 / 1 1 1 1 / 1 1 1 1 / 1 1 **1 1**

4 4 4 4 / 4 4 **4 4** / 1 1 1 1 / 1 1 **1 1**

5 5 5 5 / 4 4 **4 4** / 1 1 **1 1** / 5 5 **5 5**

2) "Quick IV" = Goes to IV in the 2nd bar

1 1 **1 1** / 4 4 **4 4** / 1 1 1 1 / 1 1 **1 1**

4 4 4 4 / 4 4 **4 4** / 1 1 1 1 / 1 1 **1 1**

5 5 **5 5** / 4 4 **4 4** / 1 1 **1 1** / 5 5 **5 5**

Soloing Over Different Turnarounds

Finally, don't forget that if we apply variations to the turnaround section (usually bars 9 through 12) and use a ii-V turnaround, those turnaround changes can be approached from either a half step above or below – just as we did with "grease" chords. So, we'd approach the minor ii from a half step below or above on the last couple of beats of bar 8 (typically the I chord). You could use the same idea when approaching the V chord, borrowing 2 beats from the end of bar 9. It can get tricky skating around these subs in faster tunes; maybe you only want to apply the half step idea when approaching the ii, and play the V straight – or play an altered scale (diminished, or double diminished for extra diabolical thrills!) over the V chord.

Two Basic 12-Bar Forms with Minor ii-V-I Turnarounds Using Half-Step/"Grease" Chord Approaches

Use the last 1 or 2 beats of the bars as shown in **bold** to approach the next chord change from a half-step below or above to create tension/release.

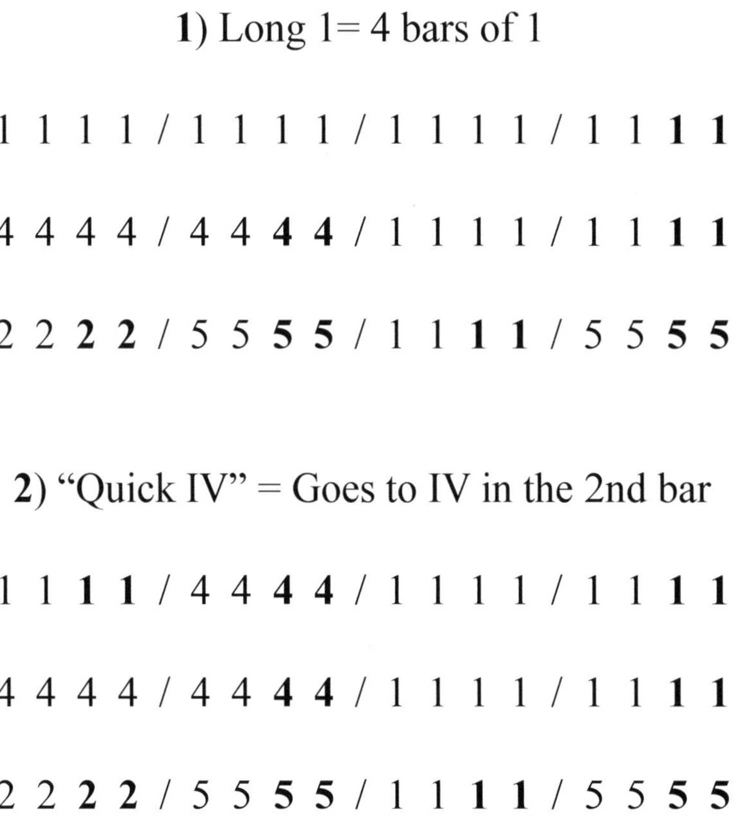

1) Long 1= 4 bars of 1

1 1 1 1 / 1 1 1 1 / 1 1 1 1 / 1 1 **1 1**

4 4 4 4 / 4 4 **4 4** / 1 1 1 1 / 1 1 **1 1**

2 2 **2 2** / 5 5 **5 5** / 1 1 **1 1** / 5 5 **5 5**

2) "Quick IV" = Goes to IV in the 2nd bar

1 1 **1 1** / 4 4 **4 4** / 1 1 1 1 / 1 1 **1 1**

4 4 4 4 / 4 4 **4 4** / 1 1 1 1 / 1 1 **1 1**

2 2 **2 2** / 5 5 **5 5** / 1 1 **1 1** / 5 5 **5 5**

Also worth mention is the “sharp-V-V” turnaround; the most recognizable example of that could be found in B. B. King’s classic, “The Thrill Is Gone”. Try using a 9th chord for the sharp-V, and an altered dominant V chord (V7 sharp-9, affectionately referred to as “The Hendrix Chord”; or a diminished chord, or an augmented chord) for the V. Use the chord tones as a template for soloing reference points and create 3 or 4-note phrases during each chords’ respective bar.

Listen to audio track 24 and try similar ideas over play-along tracks 53 and 54. Note that these play-along tracks are all in the key of C♯ minor.

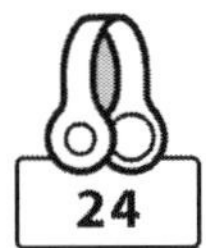

Sharp V and Altered V Chords

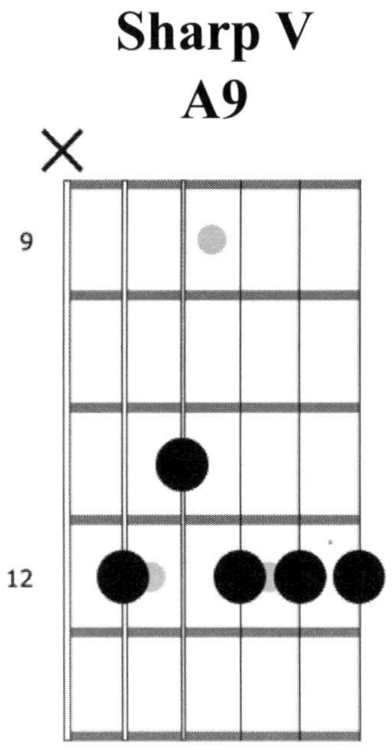

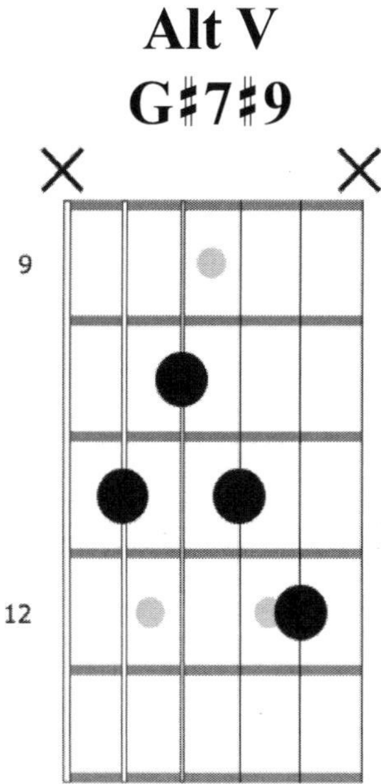

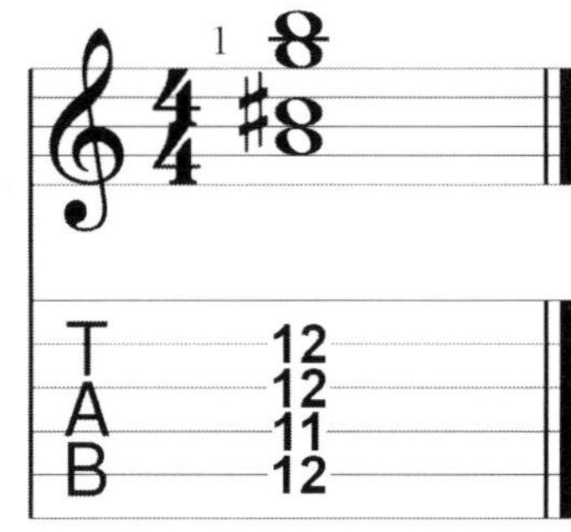

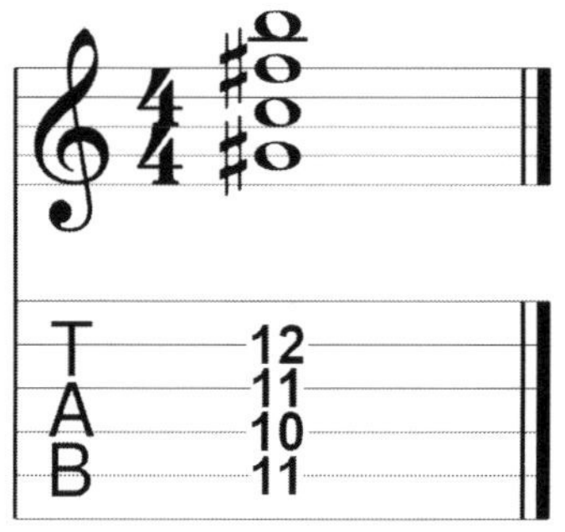

Alt V
A Dim7

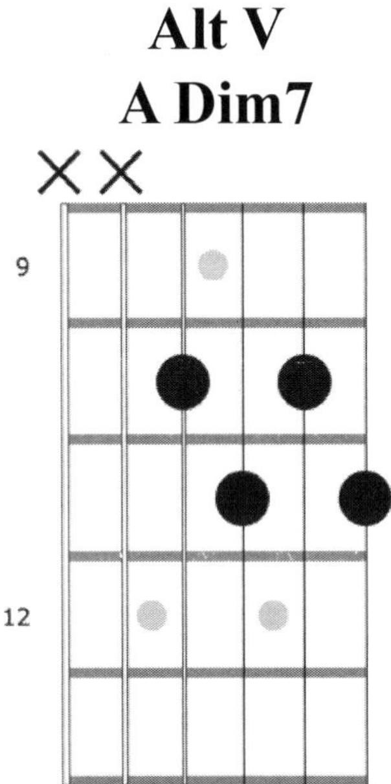

Alt V
G♯Aug

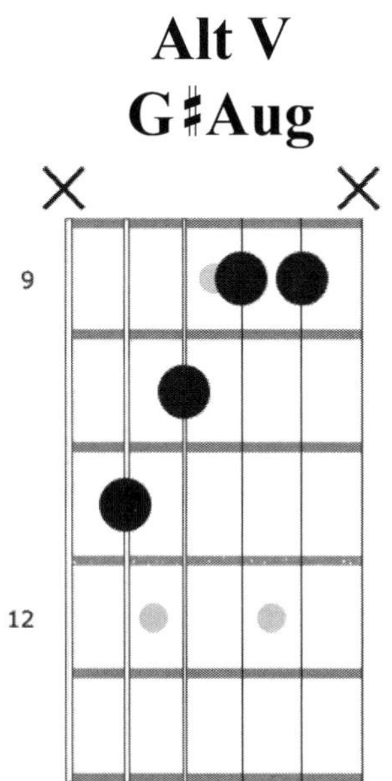

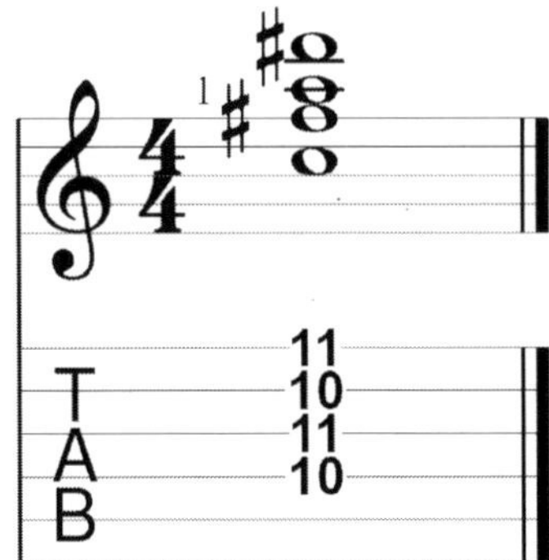

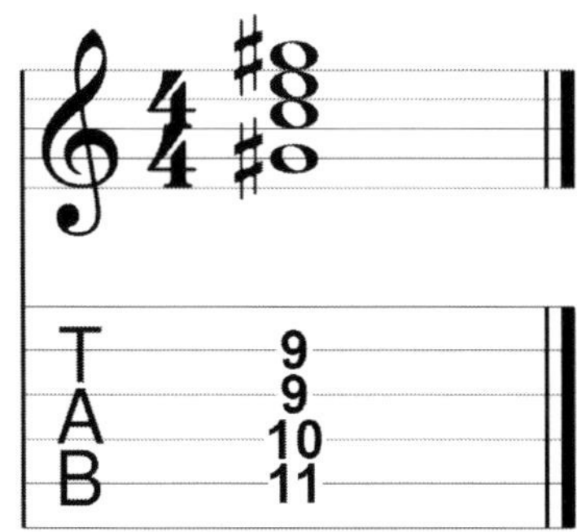

CONCLUSION

The opportunities for musical espionage are endless, and endlessly entertaining for players and listeners.

I really hope you take away some new ideas and perspectives, and maybe some inspiration from this book and the accompanying play-along tracks.

One of the things that made me want to share this stuff is that I hit a creative wall a while back, and out of a combination of boredom and a little desperation, I sought out a teacher to help me broaden my harmonic and rhythmic horizons. Initially, I left those lessons discouraged, as much of it was over my head – but one day I realized that if I just grasped one new idea, I could apply it across dozens of tunes and changes.

Take your time with this book; try to add one or two new ideas to your bag each time you experiment with the examples here. It doesn't look like rocket science, but any change to the basic, beloved 12-bar blues form was disorienting to me at first. Remember, slow and steady wins the race.

I'd also encourage you to study and digest the ii-V turnaround and check out some of the pioneers of jump blues – guys like Joe Turner, Wynonie Harris, Freddie Green, Red Prysock, and other singers and horn players, super-inspiring creators of swinging phrasing and rhythmic propulsion, and essential innovators who helped birth the most important vocabularies in blues and roots music.

Regarding the play-along tracks, please note that tracks 25 through 39 are all I-IV-V turnarounds in various feels, tempos and keys. Tracks 40-54 are more challenging; they are grouped in sets of three in a given key, with varying tempos and turnarounds. They were designed to give you a "progressive resistance" opportunity.

For those of you with DAW (digital audio workstation – *GarageBand*, etc.) software, you can adjust each track's tempo while maintaining the same key. It's like having your own band, except they stay out of your refrigerator!

I'd also like to send special thanks/acknowledgements to Daryl Tomas, transcriptionist and guitarist extraordinaire at DTGuitarStudio.com; Ric Glass, publishing and layout guru and long-time pal, at ricglass.com; Marc Ward for voice and guitar audio engineering; all the friendly folks at Mel Bay Publications; and my eternally patient wife.

Play on, Brothers and Sisters!

PLAY-ALONG TRACK LISTING 25 - 39

I / IV / V, 12-Bar Format (BPMs approximate)

25 – Stylin' & Profilin'	Blues Shuffle in G	100 bpm
26 – Blue Fool	Blues Shuffle in C	120 bpm
27 – Git It	Blues Shuffle in E	150 bpm
28 – Four on the Floor	Straight 8 Rockabilly in A	130 bpm
29 – Rockin' Out	Straight 8 Rockabilly in E	150 bpm
30 – Gone	Straight 8 Rockabilly in C	180 bpm
31 – Swing-A-Billy	Shuffle Rockabilly in B♭	160 bpm
32 – Jukin'	Shuffle Rockabilly in E	180 bpm
33 – Go Man Go	Shuffle Rockabilly in C	200 bpm
34 – Waterlogged	Surf in Am	140 bpm
35 – Turkish Twist	Surf in Em	160 bpm
36 – Horror Beach	Surf in Dm	180 bpm
37 – Hellbilly	Train Beat Country in C	180 bpm
38 – Funky Redneck	Train Beat Country in G	220 bpm
39 – Peelin' Out	Train Beat Country in E	260 bpm

PLAY-ALONG TRACK LISTING 40 - 54

Grouped In 3, By Feel – In Different Tempos and Turnarounds

40 - Butterbeans	New Orleans	I-IV-V in G	80 bpm
41 - Butterbeans	New Orleans	ii-V in G	80 bpm
42 - Butterbeans	New Orleans	ii-V in G	90 bpm
43 - Rib Tips	Jump Blues	I-IV-V in A	120 bpm
44 - Rib Tips	Jump Blues	ii-V in A	120 bpm
45 - Rib Tips	Jump Blues	ii-V in A	140 bpm
46 - Mucho Mojo	Rhumba Blues	I-IV-V in C	125 bpm
47 - Mucho Mojo	Rhumba Blues	ii-V in C	125 bpm
48 - Mucho Mojo	Rhumba Blues	ii-V in C	135 bpm
49 - Dirtsurfin'	Train Beat Country	I-IV-V in G	150 bpm
50 - Dirtsurfin'	Train Beat Country	I-IV-V in G	160 bpm
51 - Dirtsurfin'	Train Beat Country	I-IV-V in G	180 bpm
52 - Blue Funk	Minor Funky Blues	I-IV-V in C♯m	90 bpm
53 - Blue Funk	Minor Funky Blues	♯V-V in C♯m	90 bpm
54 - Blue Funk	Minor Funky Blues	♯V-V in C♯m	100 bpm